Decoupage Designs

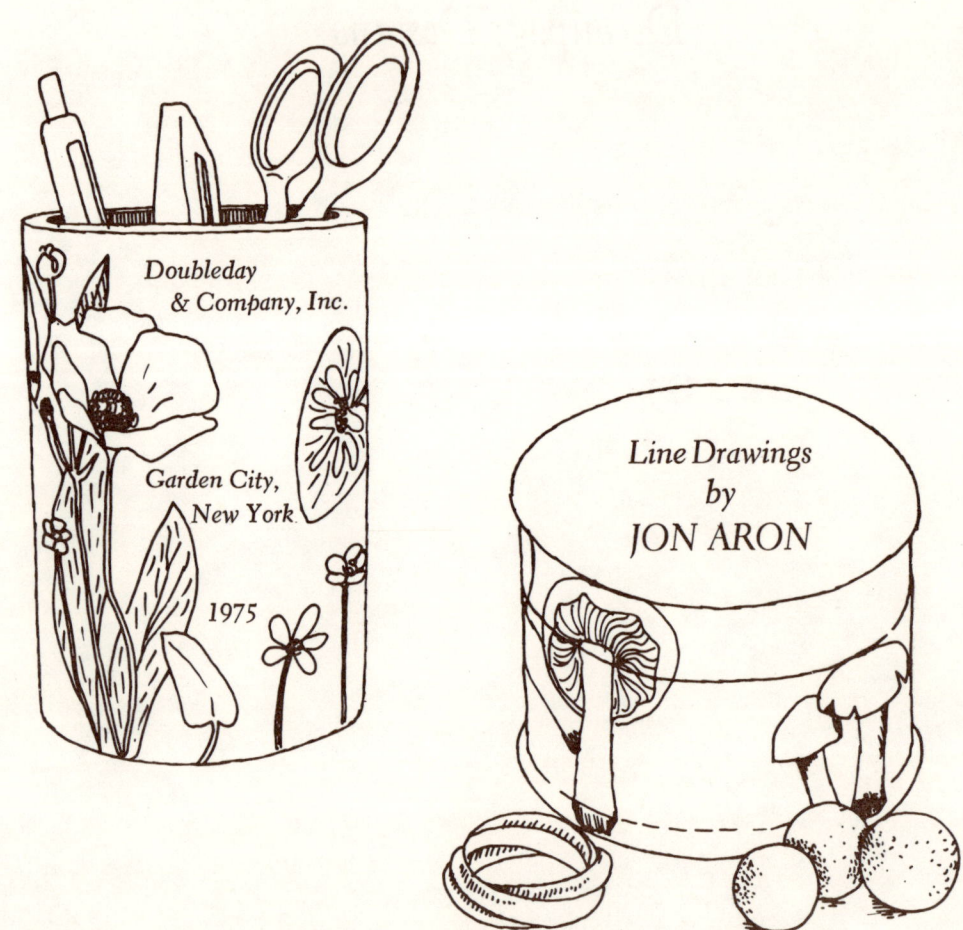

DECOUPAGE DESIGNS

by LESLIE LINSLEY

75 PROJECTS YOU CAN DO WITH COLOR PRINTS

LIBRARY OF CONGRESS CATALOGING IN PUBLICATION DATA
Linsley, Leslie.
Decoupage Designs.
1. Decoupage.   I. Title.
TT870.L54   745.54
ISBN 0-385-02720-6
Library of Congress Catalog Card Number 74–32572
Copyright © 1975 by Leslie Linsley
All Rights Reserved
Printed in the United States of America
BOOK DESIGN BY BENTE HAMANN
First Edition

For information about the decoupage supplies used in this book write to:
The Whole Works, Box 447, Westport, Conn. 06880

 contents

INTRODUCTION 9

1. THE BASICS 13

2. WORKING WITH PRINTS 27

3. WORKING WITH SHAPES 43

4. MORE IDEAS 63

Decoupage Designs

# introduction

"I'm not creative." "I never know what to do with the prints." "Where can I find good designs for decoupage?" These questions are what this book is all about. Ever since my first book was published, I have received hundreds of letters asking for sources of decoupage prints. Unfortunately it is getting more and more difficult to find usable material. Most good print shops are found only in large cities, and the prints are usually sold for framing and are often much too expensive for decoupage. Although a good source, books can also be expensive because they usually deal with only one subject such as flowers or birds, etc. You end up buying three or four books to do one project.

Magazines are out! I'll repeat that advice until you hate me, but they are the worst source. The paper is too thin and wrinkles when it is glued down, the ink usually smears when you varnish, and worst of all the printed matter shows through from the other side. Greeting cards are too thick and must be peeled (a difficult task) and often the pictures from cards, etc. aren't the right size for the object you are working on.

Of course there are ways to get around each of these obstacles and it certainly isn't my intention to make any of this seem more of a problem than it is. However, finding prints that appeal *introduction*

to you and also will work for decoupage is frequently a bewildering task for the beginner and often equally frustrating for the experienced decoupeaur. So it seemed a good idea to provide a selection of prints to work with and at the same time show a variety of ways to use them.

This workbook about decoupage design is the result. It shows how to create all kinds of projects using the prints in this book. You can make a simple key chain or an exquisite evening purse. All the prints can be arranged and rearranged in many different ways. You can combine prints for more unusual, original, one-of-a-kind pieces. I could tell you how to plunk a print down on a plaque, but I don't think you need instruction for that. However, I think you'll find a real thrill in creating your own "scene" on a plaque by mixing up prints and cutting a little off here and adding a little there.

So the purpose of this book is to get you into the spirit of what decoupage really is. I have created what I believe is a good assortment of designs for the kinds of decoupage projects you may be doing. You will find it is a very rewarding experience to create your own design rather than to use an already completed design such as a greeting card. Most of the prints in this book can also be used with others that you may have. For instance, leaves from any of the prints can always come in handy to use with something else. Or you may want a touch of color that one of the butterflies can offer. The drawings are a helpful guide, but I'm sure you can take off from there with some of your own arrangements.

In my first book, I emphasized the fact that most people don't feel creative. It's really just a matter of plunging in and doing it. If you start with a very simple design you will be quite satisfied, but after that project is finished you'll want to do something a bit more elaborate. Each time you do a box or a plaque or whatever, you will gain a little more confidence. One of my students was very timid about cutting out and arranging prints. Her first project was a small rectangular box (the nik nak box shown on page 36). She placed one flower in the center and said "There, it's done." I encouraged her to add a few leaves, another bud or two, and a butterfly. The box looked more finished and she felt that it looked better. Each project she

introduction

started after that was always approached timidly until after four or five projects she was adding her own touches with very little encouragement.

Doing anything over and over again builds confidence in your ability and judgment. That's the way it is with designing for decoupage. The more you do it, the better you become. You will also become "tuned in" and more aware of new arrangements. You will start noticing things you may have overlooked before. When I see a wildflower or a weed growing alongside a road, I often notice how it grows naturally and in relation to its surroundings. Fabrics are often an inspiration. A favorite print on a dress can spark an idea.

If you are familiar with my work you will know that I am more concerned with designing and less concerned with how many coats of varnish you use. What makes you grow and get better with decoupage is your ability to create new and interesting compositions. I've been doing decoupage for over ten years. I've practically been doing it in my sleep every night. Yet I still approach every new decoupage project with renewed excitement. Although I am familiar with how to create an interesting design, it is not from art or design courses. It's not from reading books. It is from doing over and over again. It is from being aware of my surroundings, but most of all it is a feeling. When I have arranged and rearranged my cutouts a few times, all of a sudden it is "right." It is this over and over again experimenting that is my creative process and it's what keeps this craft so alive for me.

Yet with all my experience I get stuck. I have anxious moments when I just can't make "it" happen. Hopefully this book will help you over such rough spots. My suggestions are not necessarily the best solutions for you but will provide ideas to help you begin. If you are a beginner, I hope this book will get your creative juices flowing. Perhaps you'll look at the buttercup file box, begin to make it, and midstream change a bit here and there, adding your own touch. Maybe you'll do a tiny trinket box just as I have and then go on to bigger and better projects of your own, combining prints I never thought to use together.

1. the basics

Let's Do Decoupage

This really isn't a how-to-do-decoupage book; however, I think it's important to take a little time to outline the processes of decoupage before jumping into designing.

When I teach a class I usually have my students begin with one of the smaller wooden boxes. For even a small item you must use all the necessary techniques of decoupage, but you will have the satisfaction and encouragement of a finished piece much sooner. Then as you progress to a larger box or a piece of furniture you will be familiar with all the steps and possible problems that can occur. So, the instructions that follow assume you are working on a small trinket box.

Materials Needed

Craft shops are located all over the country and usually have a good supply of decoupage materials. Art stores, hardware stores and some department stores carry supplies. Check antique shops, tag sales, thrift shops, etc. for boxes and other items to

Decoupage Designs

decoupage. Book stores often have sales on books with good illustrations. Your local paint store may have old wallpaper samples.

You will need the following:

1. An *object* to be decoupaged.
2. *Sandpaper*, such as 3M wet or dry superfine, one piece #400 and one piece #600.
3. *Paint*. I use latex or acrylic for almost all my projects, but enamel is also fine if you have it.
4. *Brush*. A natural bristle brush that can be used for painting and varnishing. This can be obtained in craft or art supply stores. The new poly brushes also work well and are very inexpensive.
5. *Varnish*. This is not shellac or lacquer. You should use a good indoor varnish. Most varnishes come in a dull matte finish, semi gloss, or very glossy for a glasslike finish.
6. *Paint thinner*, *turpentine*, or *mineral spirits* for cleaning your brush after varnishing.
7. *Antiquing mix*. This is optional and depends on your taste. I think the antiquing gives a piece character, but many people choose not to antique their work.
8. A piece of *cheesecloth* or clean rag for antiquing.
9. Small piece of #0000 *steel wool*.
10. Tiny bit of white *paste wax* such as Butcher's bowling alley wax or Johnson's furniture paste wax.
11. A good pair of sharp *cuticle scissors* is most important.
12. White *glue* such as Elmer's or Sobo.

Now you're ready to begin. With the heavy-grade sandpaper (#400), sand your box lightly just enough to make it smooth to paint. Wipe off sand "dust" and paint the box inside and out. Don't forget the bottom. Set the box aside to dry. When placing the box on a shelf to dry be sure to let it hang over the edge slightly so that air can get inside, for if air can't circulate it will take longer for this part to dry. It should be ready for another coat of paint in about fifteen minutes if you *the basics*

use a water base paint, or in twenty-four hours if you use enamel. If you are using white paint, the box will need three coats. If you use a darker color, such as green, you will find that the paint covers better and you will probably need only two coats.

While your paint dries you can begin to cut out your print. Cuticle scissors are the best for this as you will be able to cut out the most delicate designs and will find it easy to cut the hard-to-reach places, such as between leaves and buds. Hold your scissors curved away from you for best results. When doing a project, try to cut the most difficult prints first while you are most alert. As you become tired of cutting, you will be glad you saved those mushrooms for last. The better the cutting the neater your piece will be. All the white paper should be cut away even if you have to cut some of the color away to get in close enough. Your scissors should be kept sharp for a smooth professional cutting job.

When your paint is dry to the touch, sand the box inside and out with the superfine sandpaper (#600). After sanding lightly apply a second coat of paint to the box. When sanding, do not rub too hard or you will sand your first coat of paint right off. When the paint dries, sand again and if needed apply a third coat of paint. Lightly sand your final coat of paint when it is thoroughly dry. If you are working on a larger box, you may want to line the inside with wallpaper rather than painting it.

Now you are ready for your designs. Arrange the cutout pieces in a pleasing way on the box. Remember to save one of the designs for the inside, if it has not been lined. Apply a small amount of glue on the back of a cutout piece. Spread the glue evenly over the back of the cutout print and set it in place on your box. Press it down firmly with your hand. With a damp sponge wipe off all excess glue that oozes out from the sides. Continue to apply each cutout this way. The designs can go from top to bottom and later can be cut with a razor blade where the lid and base come together.

When you glue very delicate stems and leaves it is a bit trickier. If you dilute the glue with a drop or two of water it will be easier to handle. Brush the glue on the back of each

Decoupage Designs

cutout. This will eliminate handling it any more than necessary. If you have any glue on your fingers, wash your hands before picking up the design. Know beforehand exactly where you want to place the design. Once in place, it is almost impossible to change it.

When all your prints are glued on, you are ready to varnish. Varnish the lid and bottom of the box separately. Dip the brush into the can of varnish and apply it to your box right over the design. Start at the center and work toward each outer edge. Then varnish around the outer rim. Be sure that you do not have too much varnish on your box or it will drip down the sides. A thin coat of varnish is better than a very thick one, for then each coat will be more perfect and will dry to a hard finish.

When the box is dry, turn it over and do the bottom as well as the inside of the top. Now set your box aside, preferably on an out of the way shelf so that it can dry for twenty-four hours. After the varnish has dried thoroughly apply two more coats exactly the same way. Each coat should dry overnight or all day before applying the next coat. After three coats of varnish sand the box very lightly with your superfine sandpaper (#600). Do not sand with a heavy hand, as you might sand right through to the print. The sanding is simply to remove any roughness or air bubbles that may have formed on the surface.

Continue to apply five or six coats of varnish, sanding between each coat. With a small box five or six coats of varnish are often enough. When working on a larger piece, such as a purse that will be handled frequently, you may want to apply as many as fifteen or twenty coats. I like a slightly raised surface so that you can feel the design when you run your hand over the finish. This effect is determined by the number of coats of varnish you apply. The more varnishing you do the more your designs will be covered, thus producing a surface that will be mirror smooth.

If you decide to antique, apply the last coat of varnish and *do not sand.* The antiquing mix can be purchased premixed or you can mix your own with an umber pigment purchased at the art store. Coat your entire box with antiquing using your paintbrush. With the clean cloth wipe most of the antiquing away, leaving accents around your design and in corners or

16

8.

9.

10.

11.

12.

13.

14.

the basics

around the outer edge. The antiquing should create a very subtle effect. Set the box aside and try not to get fingerprints on it. In a couple of hours the antiquing will be dry.

Apply a final coat of varnish over the entire box. Let this dry overnight. When thoroughly dry, wet your fine sandpaper slightly and sand the box inside and out. Then with your steel wool rub over the box to smooth your surface even more. Wipe off the particles from the steel wool with a clean cloth and apply a thin coat of furniture paste wax. This should dry in about ten minutes. Buff and rub inside and out with a clean cloth until your box takes on a shine. This finish should glow like a fine piece of furniture.

If you are working on a large box or a plaque, you can glue a piece of felt to the underside to protect your furniture or wall. This can be applied by spreading white glue on the bottom of the box or back of the plaque and laying the piece of felt right on top. Smooth it down with your hand. Trim any excess felt with your cuticle scissors or razor blade.

Now, on with designing for decoupage.

2. working with prints

The first decision you must make is what to decoupage. There are hundreds of objects you can do. Decoupage can be done on wood, metal, ceramic, stone, and under glass, so your choice is almost limitless. The boxes, plaques, containers, trays, etc. in this book are some suggestions based on objects available from craft shops or items you may already have in your home. In this chapter I've taken the same object and designed it in many different ways. Five different shapes are used so that you can get a feeling for designing on a flat object as well as on a round or oval shape. Some of the projects are easier than others so both a beginner or advanced decoupage designer can work on the same type of box although with different designs. This way you can start cautiously with simple prints, learn the technique, and then go on to more complex arrangements. When I refer to prints used they are from the color sections.

File Box

Any one object can be designed in many different ways. You've just bought a box or found an old metal file box in the attic. Now what to do with it? Since there are all kinds of people with as many different tastes everyone wouldn't look at the same box in the same way. A file box made of metal or wood can be designed in a variety of ways. Almost any one of the prints in this book can work well on a box of approximately this size and shape. This particular box holds 3×5-inch file cards and could be used for recipes in the kitchen or addresses on a desk. The mushroom box is the easiest to do. The mushroom prints (※1 and 2) are simple to cut out and there is not much designing skill involved. A white background color looks well

working with prints

with the brown mushrooms. When you are finished you can line the box with a complementary piece of wallpaper or wrapping paper.

The pink flowers (※3 and 4) are slightly more difficult to cut out because the delicate stems must be handled carefully. However, using sharp cuticle scissors you will be able to get close to the stems. There are many ways to arrange these delicate flowers. I have given you one suggestion here, but if you push the designs around on the box a bit you may find another that you prefer. A soft green is a nice background color. White looks good as a background for all the prints, but often another color gives you variety.

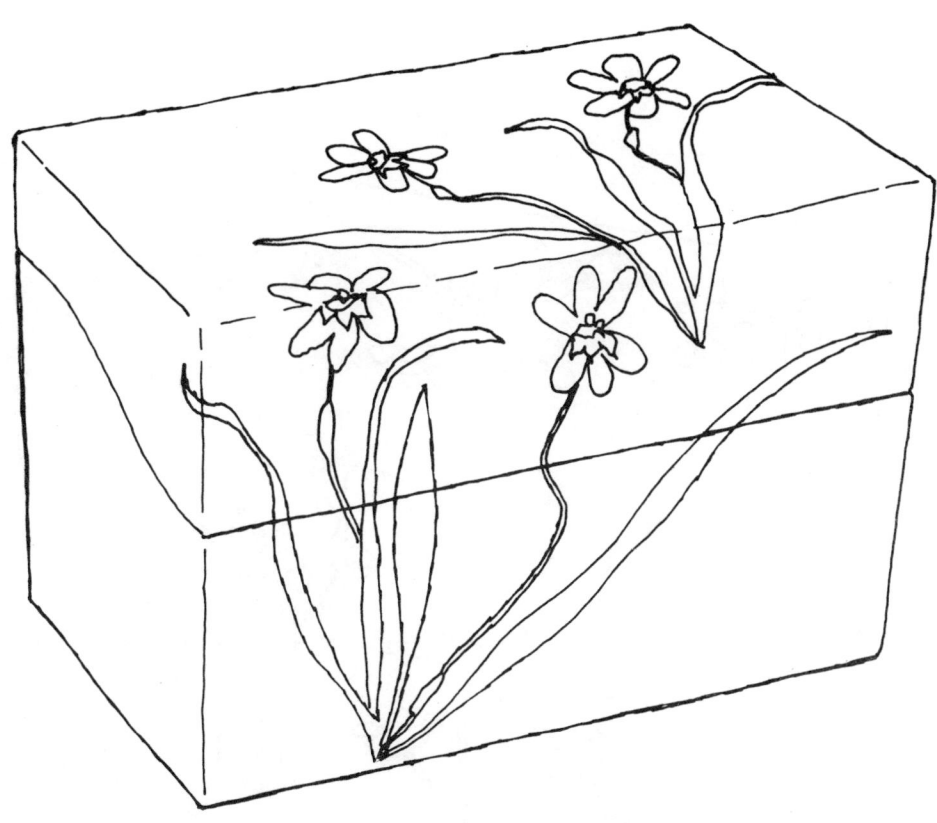

Decoupage Designs

The buttercups (#5 and 7) look bright and sunshiny for a kitchen file box. I have used these flowers with a white painted background and also with a yellow background, and I cannot make up my mind which I like best. Both are very pretty. The large flowers are placed on the box as is. Don't forget to cut out all white spaces. You have to do an especially good cutting job when placing a design on a color other than white because the white paper shows up. After I cut the single, smaller flowers, I pasted them on the box one at a time so that they come together at the stems forming a cluster. I arranged the flowers so that they aren't too formal-looking. These are wildflowers and should look as though they are growing at random. If you make this box you might place a design on each side or have part of the stem from the lower left flower begin on the side and come around to the front. A leaf or a single butterfly could add a nice touch to the back. If you want to sign your name to your piece, use India ink and sign it before you varnish.

Trinket Box

This trinket box is a good starter project because it is small and you see results right away. It also makes a great gift for anyone of any age. Any small box that you can find will do. The designs that I've chosen for this little round box are easy to cut out and not complicated to arrange on an item. When you have all the pieces cut out, try using them in different ways. If you save one of the designs for the inside it makes a nice surprise when someone opens the box. Any item that has a top and bottom that fit together should be designed as a whole. In other words, leave the top on when you are gluing the cutouts in place. Once you have completed the box you can cut across the print with a razor blade where the top and bottom come together. This way your design will always match up perfectly. You might even want to put a small cutout on the bottom.

These pink flowers (※9) are rose hips and were inspired by the Nantucket wildflowers that grow all over the island. This print would be especially nice in a bedroom and the little box could hold rings. Use a pale blue or white background for this design.

31

Decoupage Designs

I often place mushrooms (※1) on a white background, but they also look well on yellow. Use the beetle (※1), and glue it on top of one of the mushrooms for a special touch. Arrange the mushrooms on the box before applying them with glue. Be sure all the mushrooms are evenly spaced around the box.

The dandelion and black-eyed Susan print (※11) that I used on the third trinket box gives an entirely different feeling. Here this print is used effectively on a tiny three-inch box and later in the book you will see the same design, combined with other prints, and used on a wastebasket and a long pencil box. This is one of my favorite prints because it is very versatile and the colors are so vibrant. This box shows a more integrated look because the flowers flow into one another creating a "scene" even on this little object. If they are out of proportion, don't worry about it. The advantage to decoupage is that you can take creative liberties with design, and you don't have to be an artist to do it. I often place little characters walking through fields of giant flowers. Call it a fantasy scene.

The mushroom trinket box is the easiest to do here and the black-eyed Susan box the most difficult. The red flower in this print takes some time to cut out and must be done carefully so that you don't tear one of the buds off. When applying these designs to the box, place a dab of glue on the back of

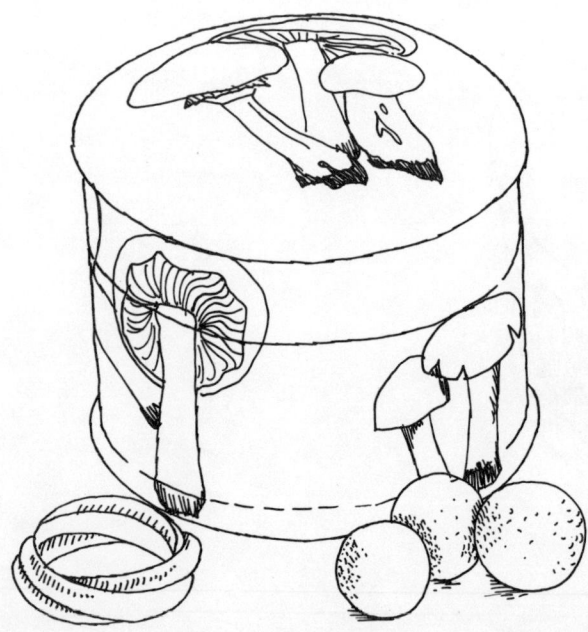

32

working with prints

each print and carefully lay it in position. If you dilute the glue slightly with a drop of water it will make it a little easier to handle the red flower.

The large black-eyed Susan on the top of the box is a separate piece. The leaves are attached to it and are another cutout. Glue the leaves around the base of the box first. Then glue the flower down by placing the stem at the root of the leaves. Work it up over the ridge and onto the top of the box. Be sure all edges are securely pasted down. If you have trouble cutting the butterfly antennae, draw them on the box using India ink.

When working on a three-dimensional object, such as a box, you should take into consideration all sides. Each side should not be isolated as a separate project, but should be integrated into an over-all design. Also you will have a more delightful box if you work on it as a whole.

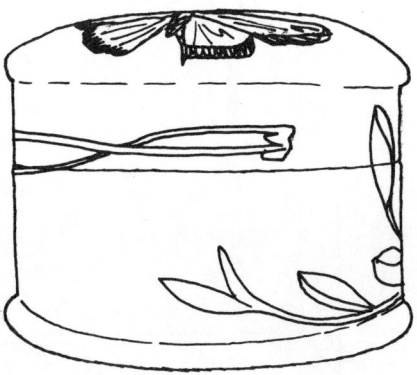

Plaques

Plaques are very popular for decoupage as they are easy to do and are a good way to learn the process. Too often plaque projects involve placing a print on the board and varnishing it, but a plaque has much more potential for creativity. But remember, a plaque should be approached differently from a three-dimensional box. With a plaque you are working with one surface and creating a composition that is viewed in only one way.

working with prints

Here are some suggestions for unique plaques and later in the book you'll find others. The purple flowers (✻12) are used on an invitation plaque. The same could be done with a wedding invitation, anniversary, birth announcement, or a photograph.

The thistle (✻6) and iris prints (✻8) make a lovely pair. The colors complement one another and the touch of pink in the flowers and blue in the butterfly add accent. The background color is sky blue. It could also be white.

The thistle takes a while to cut, but you can do it a little at a time. Cut from the center outward so you have something to grip while cutting the lacy leaves. This is not a cutting job for a beginner. To make this print design on the plaque I cut the stem apart. The piece that I cut from the left side was then placed on the other side. Later you will see it cut apart and designed differently.

Nik Nak Box

Square boxes seem to be the easiest to find if you haven't already got one. The one that I used here is 4×5½ inches and is hinged. It is a good size and can be designed in a variety of ways. The mushrooms would be a simple solution. You can place a mushroom right on the front where the top and bottom close together or put a clasp on the front of a box and arrange the mushrooms to go around the clasp. The little elf smoking his pipe could be placed right above a catch on the front.

The leaves look quite nice on everything, but more difficult than the others to cut out. However, after you have cut a few of the prints you will find this a breeze. But I don't often recommend it as a first project. One print (※14) is all that is needed for this size box. There are enough leaves in this print to use on the box so that they hang from the top, across the

working with prints

front, and on both sides. This is what I mean by integrating the entire object. The color of the red berries could be picked up on the inside by lining it with red paper. A white background makes a really striking setting for the green and red colors. If you cut the stems first and then the leaves, it will be easier to manage.

The design didn't fit exactly as it was, so I cut the leaves apart. The large berry cluster was placed at the end of one of the leaf branches across the top. If a print doesn't work just as it is, change it to fit the object.

This nik nak box was designed with the jungle cat print (※10). This is a very easy box to make. There are only three pieces to cut out and they are quite large. One of the cats was placed so that it appears to be coming around the corner. For more interest you could add some tall grasses by using the stems from print (※3). An alternative might be to place a few of the leaves coming down from the top above the tiger's head.

Decoupage Designs

Using only one set of buttercups (#5) on this nik nak box you have another concept. The largest flower is placed over to the left coming from the bottom of the front. It is interesting to have the design begin at the bottom of the front and continue up over the top. The smaller flowers could be arranged so that they also grow from the sides up onto the top. This is an easy print to use, but the results will look quite professional.

Remember also that when the glue is on the back of the cutout, it is quite pliable and a branch or flower can be curved slightly without any trouble. It will look perfectly natural.

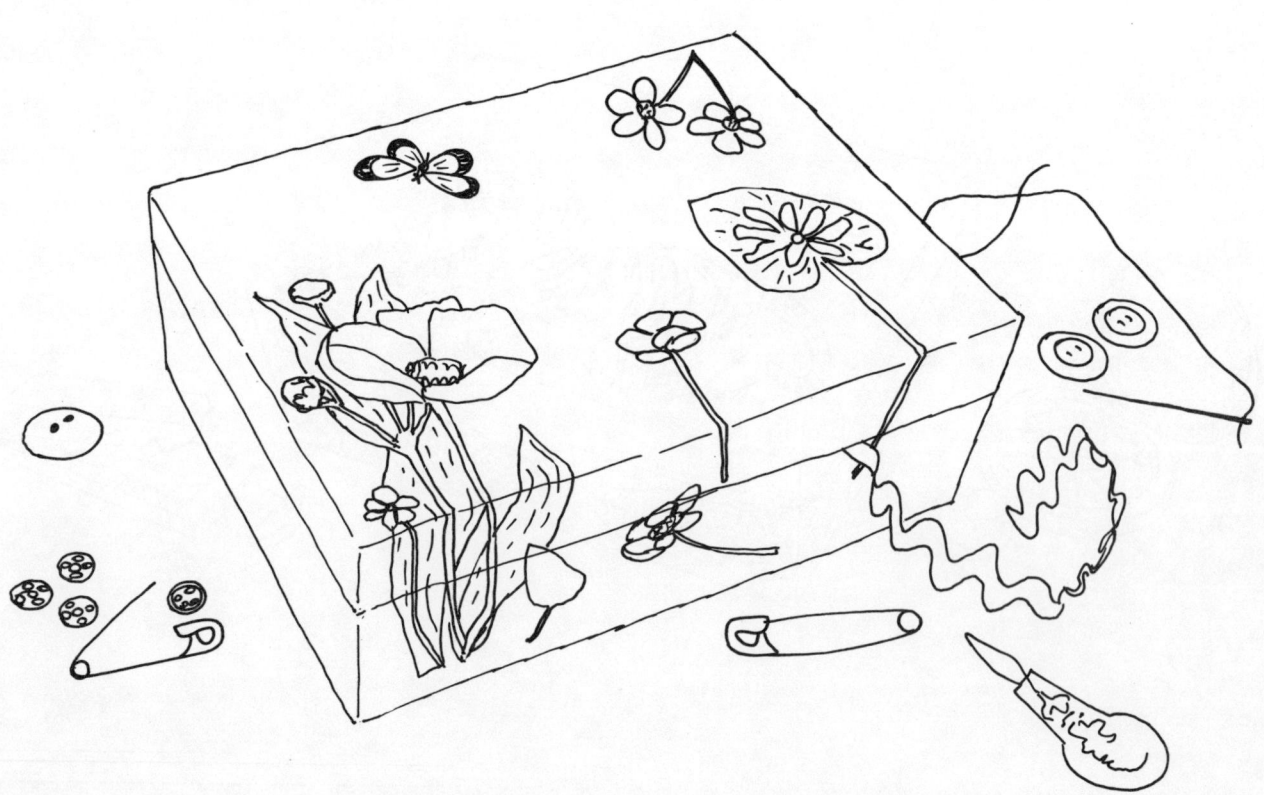

Catchall

These cylinders are about 4½ inches high and are made of wood. However, ceramic pots, a drinking glass, or cheese crocks are about the same size. You face an entirely different design problem when working with a cylindrical object. The pink flowers, print (※4), were used here. Only one set was used and arranged in a cluster. The long stem was placed at the base of the vase and curved so that it wraps around the side. You can use more of the flowers if you want to have a continuous design that flows completely around the sphere.

The buttercup print (※7) was used on the cup. This time the flowers are growing straight up from the bottom all in a row. They do not seem stiff on this object because the shape of the item is curved. One of the designs was placed so that it comes down and around from the top rim. You can see part of it coming around from the right side.

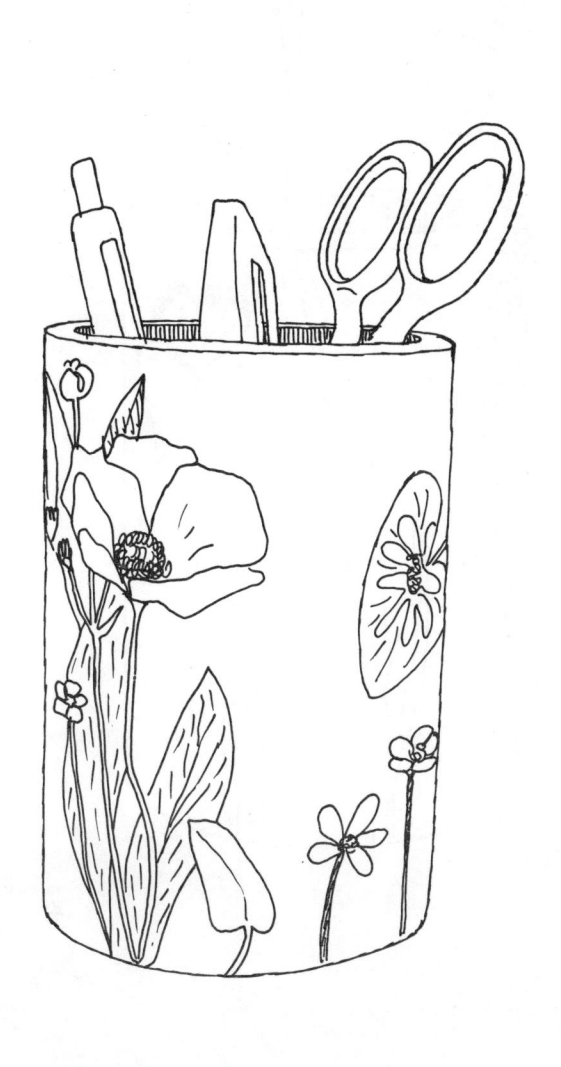

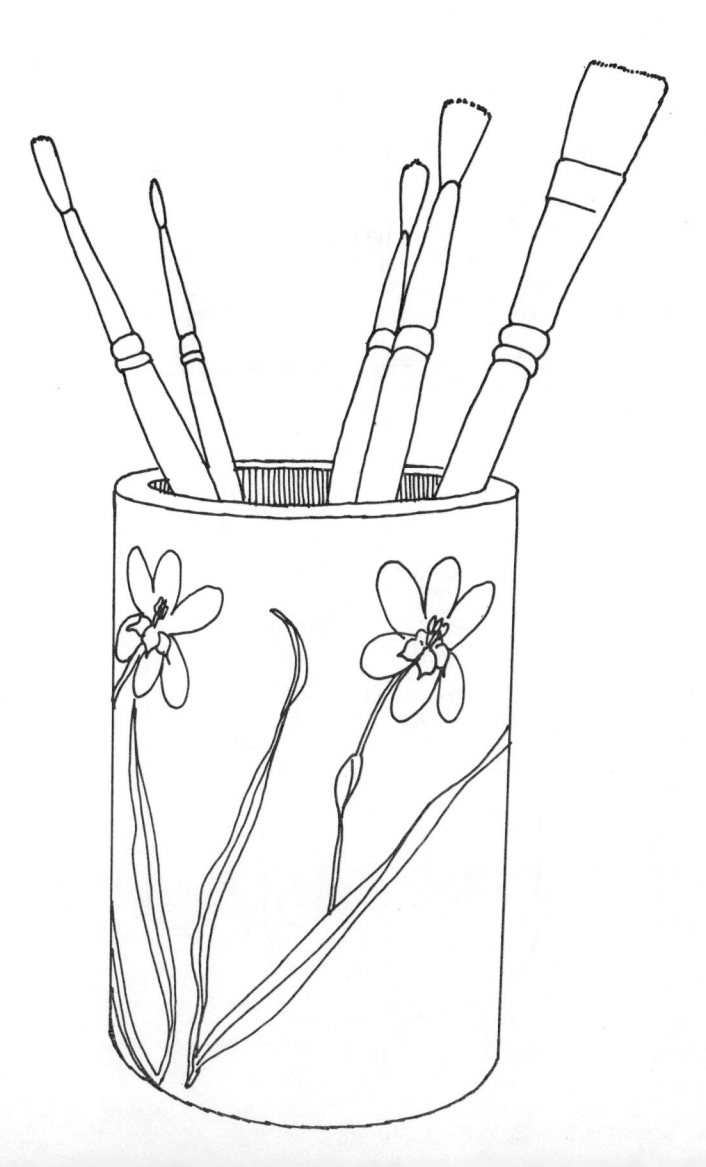

Decoupage Designs

If the large flower is too long for the cup, cut the excess off from the bottom. The main part of the flower will still be intact. The background color used here is orange and the inside is yellow to match the flowers.

The iris print (#8) was cut out and applied so that it is evenly spaced around the cup. Since the flowers are taller than the cup an alteration is required. The pink flower is shortened where the leaf and stem form a "V". The stem that was cut off is slivered to create a few blades of grass. The iris stem and leaf are also shortened. The design looks well on a blue or white background. Use one color on the outside and a contrasting color inside. The rim on the top is prettiest when it is painted with the contrasting inside color.

working with prints

Armillary sphere (#21) didn't fit as is on the catchall. Cut out the outline of the sphere for this project. The color of this print looks well on the natural wood or on a wood-stained background. If you have a container that should be painted, use a sand color. Cut the band from the top of the print and place it on the inside rim of the container. This makes a great pencil holder for a desk.

The tiger (#10) makes a very simple design all by itself. One of the other cats could be placed on the inside or you may prefer to paint the inside. Yellow and orange are good colors here. However, I like a sand color for a natural background. A wood container can be left natural or stained with a wood stain before applying the cutout.

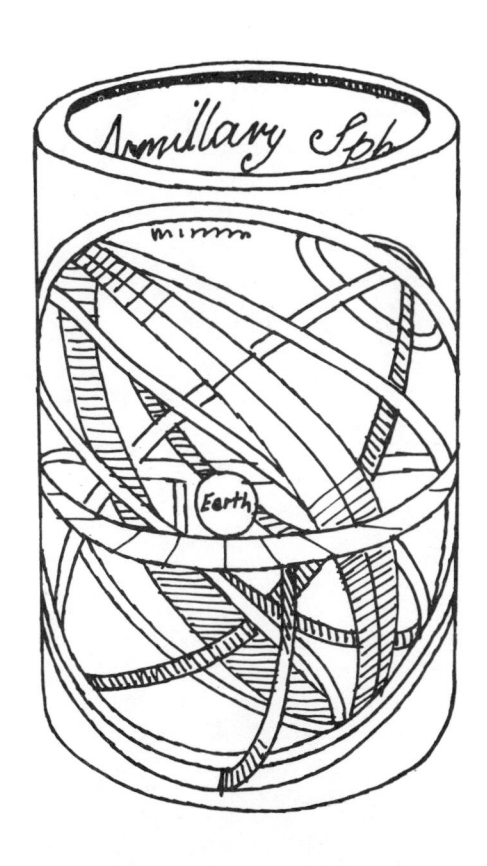

3. working with shapes

How often have you found a lovely print and not known what to do with it? Almost all prints for decoupage can be used in a variety of ways. It is often fun to try various arrangements of the same print on different shapes and sizes.

The most fun involved with the art of decoupage is in creating new designs. Don't hesitate to try many different arrangements. Sometimes you'll spend an hour or more cutting out a print and then find you can't use it because it was all wrong for the item you intended. It's important to understand that this happens often. If it doesn't look right, put it aside to use on something else. Or perhaps you can use part of it. When you take the time to make it just right you will feel more satisfied in the end. Don't rush this step. Get the most out of it.

Daisies (#16)

Wooden Egg Cup

This is a little wooden egg cup. The cutouts have been designed so that they each start at the base and extend upward. Since the flowers are different heights they come up onto the "bowl" part of the cup in a random pattern. This is usually the way you find daisies when they are growing wild. If the background color is a pale blue it will set them off as if they were growing against the sky. Use the flower without petals for the inside. It should go around the inside. This cup is painted green inside.

Trinket Box

My favorite box again. The daisies can be arranged many ways on this box. They can grow around the base or straight up and over the top. Save one of the flowers for the inside or use one of the butterflies from another print. Mustard-colored paint makes an unusual background.

Napkin Rings

Napkin rings make a terrific first project. They can be done very quickly and are an unusual gift. There are enough daisies to place one on the front of each of four rings. Use a contrasting color inside. Yellow is a nice color for these.

Stamp Dispenser

This stamp dispenser is my own designed box and gives you an idea of how to design with an unusual shape. When cutting the daisies, cut one side of each petal (say the right side), then cut all the petals on the left side. When you have jagged edges or petals to cut out this will make it more efficient and you won't have any rough edges.

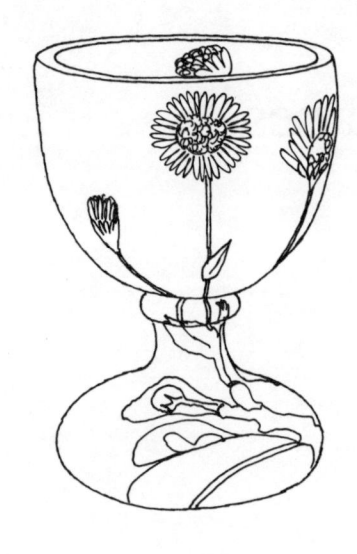

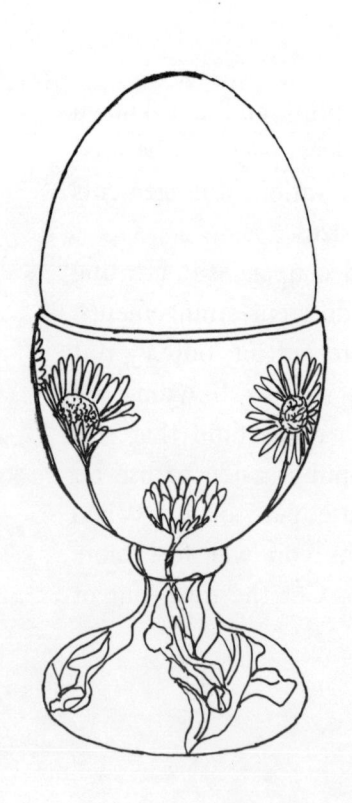

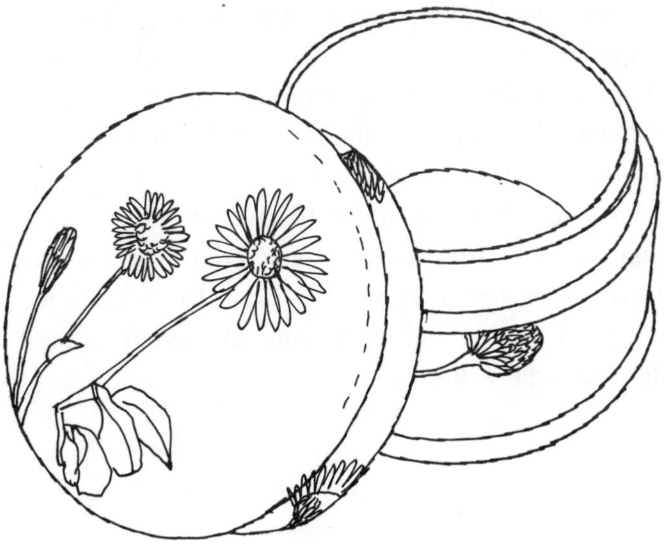

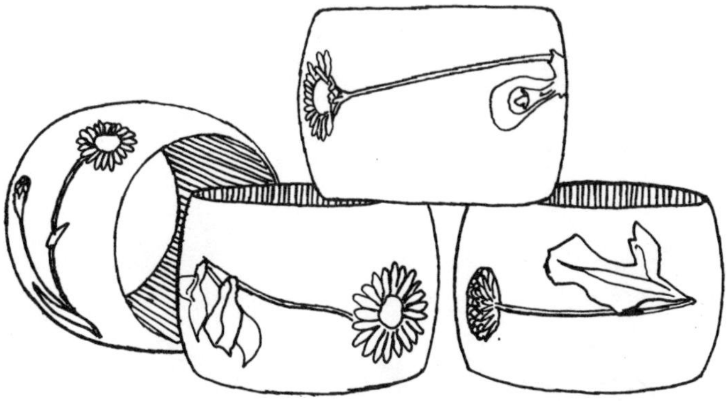

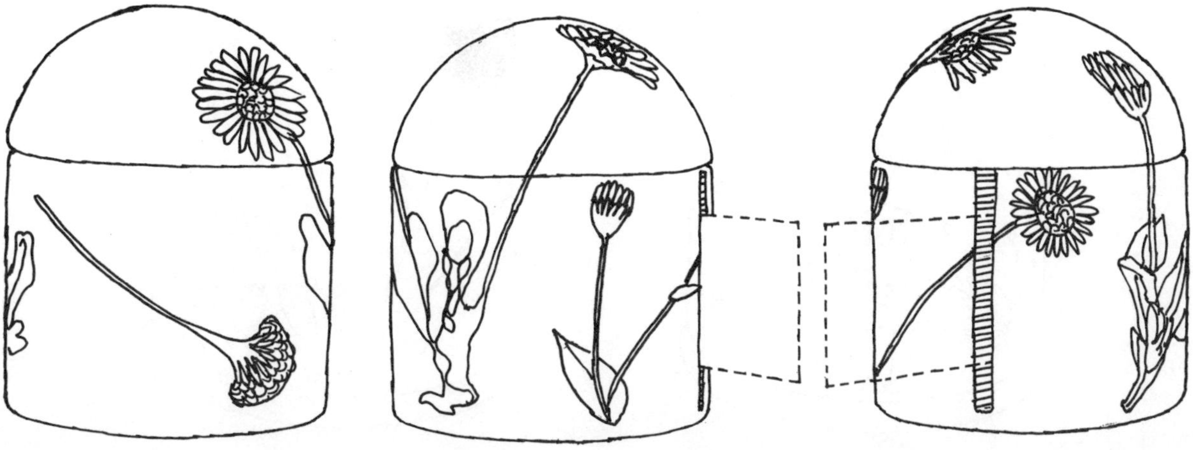

Cosmetic Cup

This little wooden cup is only 3 inches high and I've made it to hold cosmetics, but it can be a catchall of any sort. If you have a little china or ceramic cup it could make a sweet holder designed with daisies. Since they were a little too tall for this cup I designed them so that they curved or leaned to either side. Don't be afraid to cut off leaves or buds and rearrange. One of the flowers was severed from its leaves and the leaves were added to another daisy to make it fit better. Look at print (※16) and the picture on the left and see if you can discover what I did.

Purple Buds (#12)

The purple buds can be designed on small or large objects and work on flat as well as round items. I've already shown you how to use the purple buds on a plaque, but that is only one use. Perhaps you don't want to make a plaque but you like the design. Well, how about candlesticks or napkin rings? Maybe a ceramic egg cup. I have even used the same design on a trinket box and once again on the front of a small dresser.

Card Box

Combine the loose sprigs of buds so that they flow together across the box. A butterfly can be added coming from the side. This could also be done on a recipe box. This box has an ivory background color.

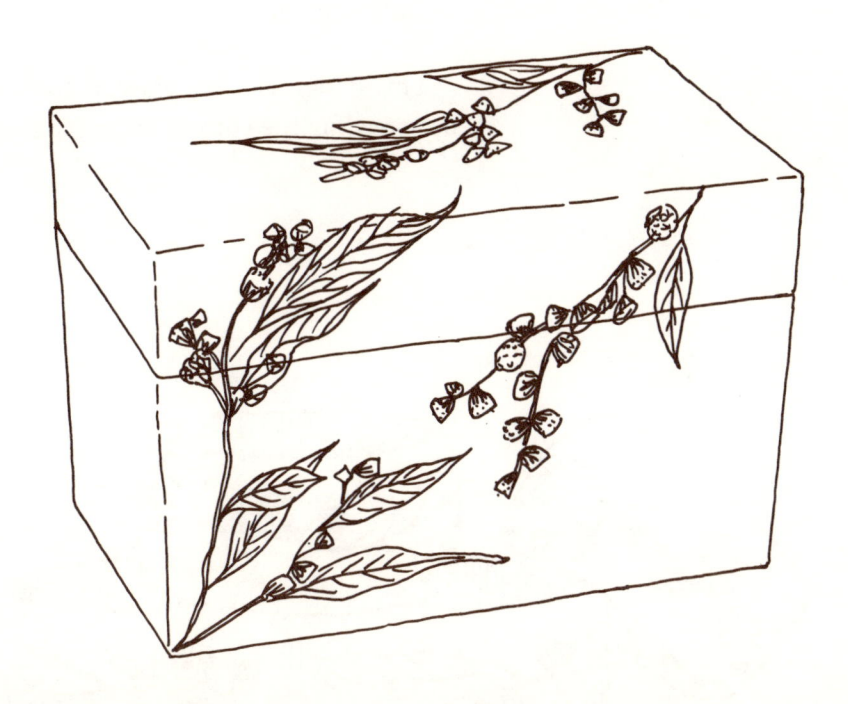

Napkin Rings

These napkin rings are smaller than the ones I used for the daisies. There are enough cutouts to make six rings from this print. Apply the design coming around the ring with the leaves extending over to the inside. These napkin rings have an ivory color background with soft green inside.

Frame

With the frame it was necessary to adapt the design by cutting off the large leaves to make it fit. A leaf is added at the base of the stem where it looked bare. Use the cut off leaves elsewhere. Never, never throw anything away. *Everything can be used.*

Ceramic Egg Cup

This ceramic egg cup did not have to be painted as it was already an off-white color. Combine the buds with the larger stems and leaves so that they sprawl around the cup.

Switchplate

This design can be adapted to double or triple switchplates by spreading the cutouts apart for a more airy design.

49

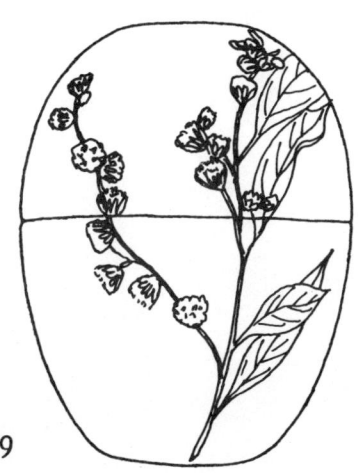

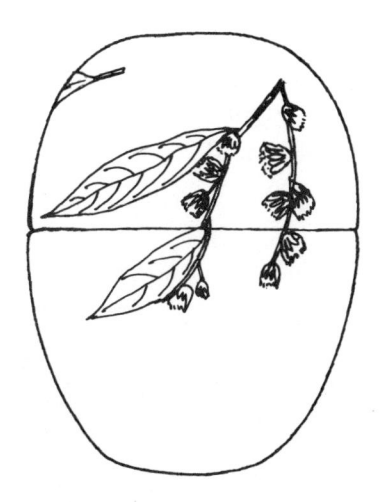

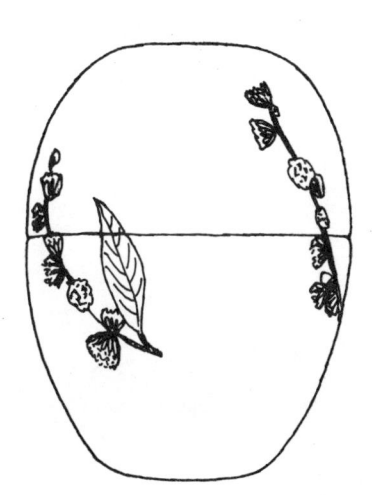

Dandelion Prints (#11 & 15)

Egg Cup

This is another wooden egg cup. Here the background color is bright red. This is a very simple project and is made with only the one dandelion, eliminating the other flowers in this print. The bright yellow against the red is very cheery on a breakfast table.

Key Chains

These key chains are made from thin chips of wood. One has a hole screwed through it. The other has a brass ring screwed into the top for the chain to go through. For these projects you only need a small part of the print. The last two leaves were cut from the trailing stem and placed at the base of the stem along with the black-eyed Susan. The background color is white. The curved key holder is painted yellow. This one makes use of the dandelion in the same print. Cut off the bottom part of the stem, apply the large leaf, and over this apply only the top part of the red flower. The small red flower adds just the right touch of color. You can then place the butterfly on the back for a complete project.

Letter Holder

This is a square open box that can be used for letters. The entire print is used on this box. The two flowers are combined with the leaves so that they become one plant. The background color is yellow. A pale yellow sets off the orange and vibrant yellow of the design.

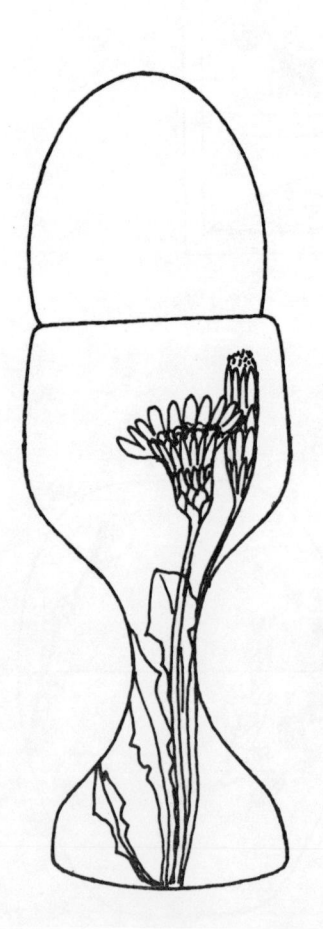

51

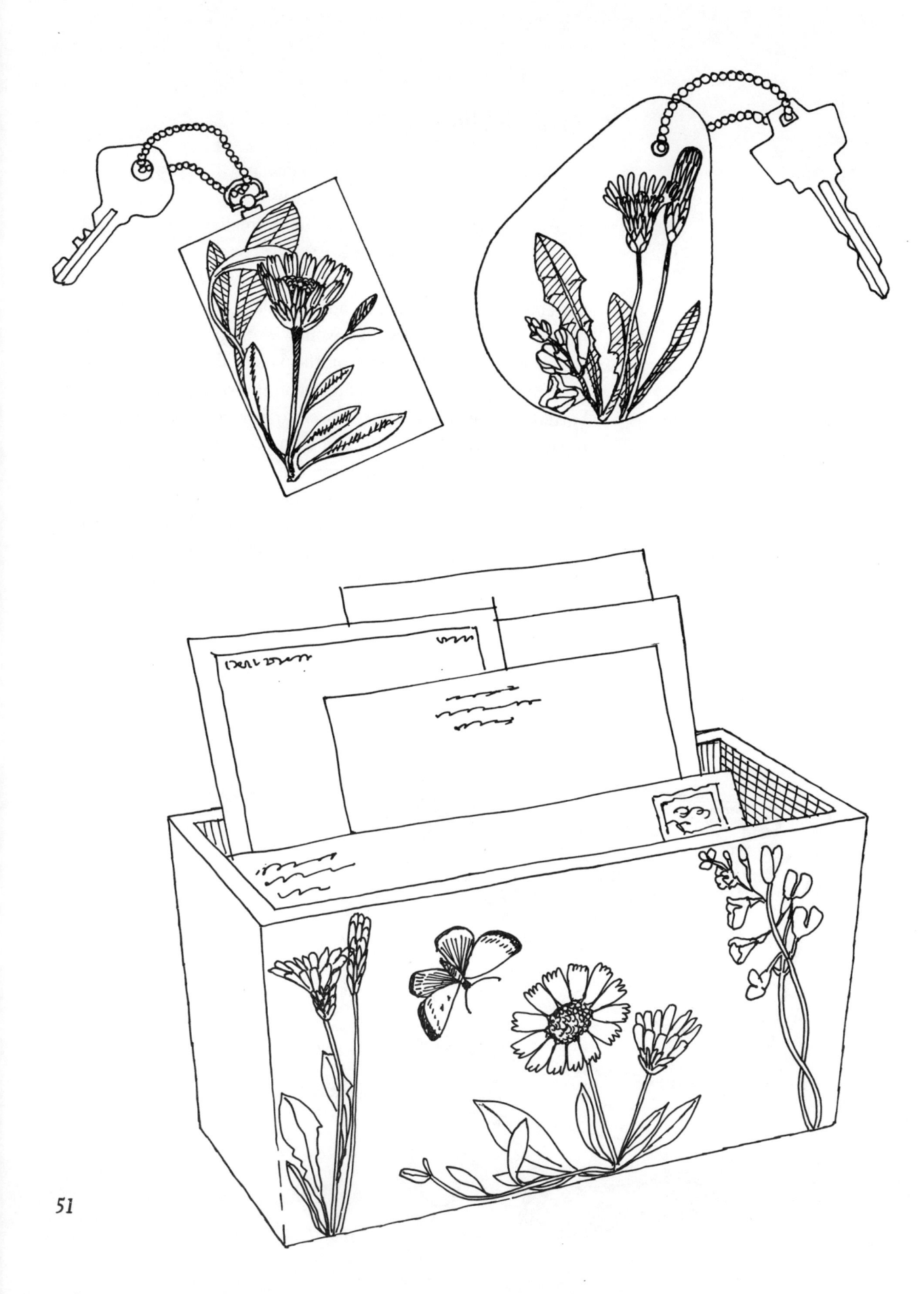

Nik Nak Box

When I designed the letter holder and the trinket box on page 33 I used the red flower in this print. You can see how different parts of the print look on a small trinket box, a key holder and a letter box or this nik nak box. The dandelion was not used on the trinket box and this time I have left the red flower off. If you want to add it, place it across the front. Another way to arrange this would be to place the dandelion at the bottom of the front of the box and extend it up and over the top. With the arrangement shown here I placed the butterfly going toward the flower to balance the design. The orange color in the butterfly can be used inside. A pastel orange paint is a good background for this design. When antiqued, a soft orange color becomes subdued. The effect is a subtle background for the bright yellow and orange colors of the print. Be sure to cut away the very tiny white space at the base of the trailing leaves. If not cut out, it will show up on a colored background.

Combining Prints

Address Ovals

This is an oval piece of pine that I made for my front door. This time print (※14) is used on an oval rather than a square item. Cut it apart so that it fits with your numbers or name. Use India ink for the letters. When the designs are wet with glue they can be curved slightly so that the design won't be so stiff on this curved shape.

Decoupage Designs

I don't usually suggest taking a large print and cutting it up just for a flower or leaf. This is because you can sometimes destroy a very beautiful print that whole could be used elsewhere. For instance, on the address oval I used a couple of the flowers, stems, and leaves from the large bouquet (#19). I could probably find other designs that would work just as well if I wanted to save the bouquet to use as a whole. It is quite lovely as is for a purse, tray, or on a box. However, if they are exactly right in size, shape, and color and you would love them on the front door you should cut it up. Play around with the designs so that you can get the most out of them.

The leaf with the berries is from the bird print (#23). The berries match the color of the rabbit's jacket and make a nice balance for the over-all dominating blue. The background is white.

Name Plaque

This plaque is for a child's bedroom door. The background is pale pink and the print is (※9). A butterfly from any of the prints can be included. Use India ink for the letters.

Mini Plaques

You can have a lot of fun making these plaques for a child's room. Three prints were combined, print (#11) and prints (#13 and 17). The plaque with the rabbit uses the trailing leaves overhead and the dandelion is cut down to size. Remember what I said, "Throw nothing away!" Take the stem that you cut from the dandelion and make slivers of it for the grass.

working with shapes

When I cut off the stem from the red flower that is forming a shade for Ms. Frog, I placed it in the lower left corner for the hen to stomp across. The rest of the grass was cut from the leftover leaf of the dandelion and the stem of the large black-eyed Susan.

The full round flower then becomes the sun for the hen. Now you're getting the hang of what I mean by designing your own plaques.

Progressive Designing

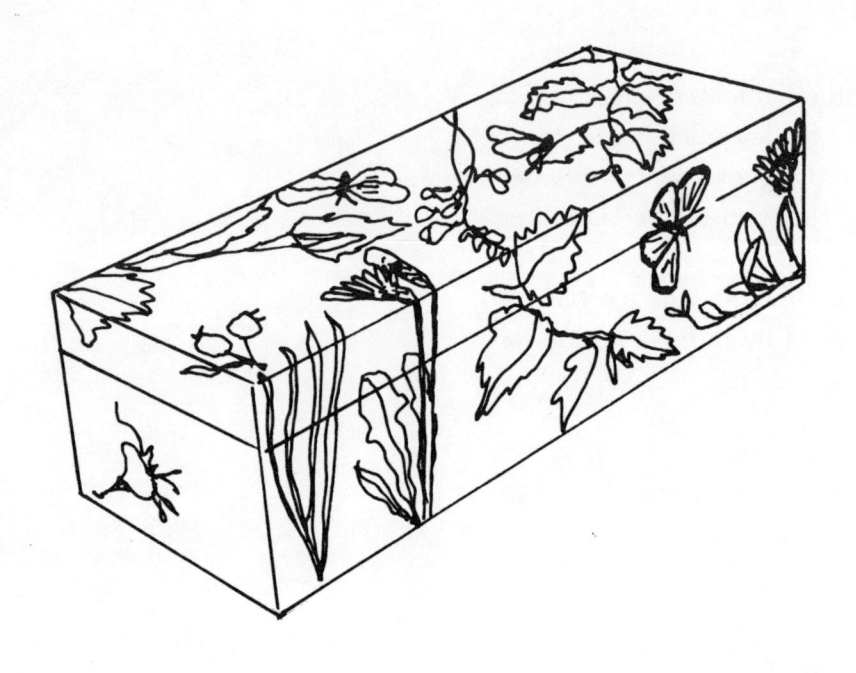

Progressive designing is starting out with a simple object and one or two cutouts and little by little creating an over-all pattern. The first design, though unadorned and simple enough for a beginner to tackle, should look complete. By adding a little more to the original box, the design becomes a bit more involved, and it goes from being a beginner's project to a more advanced project. If still more prints are added, it becomes a very professional-looking design. This does not mean that the simple box looks unprofessional, but it is fun to see how far one can carry a design on one item. Combining prints takes some practice, but most of the prints in this book can be combined for larger projects than I have presented for you.

The long pencil box that I call an "anything" box is 8 inches long, 3 inches wide, and 2½ inches high. It is made of wood and hinged. I often put a clasp on the front for interest. Notice with this box I used print (※14). This time I didn't cut it apart too much. The background color is white, which

working with shapes

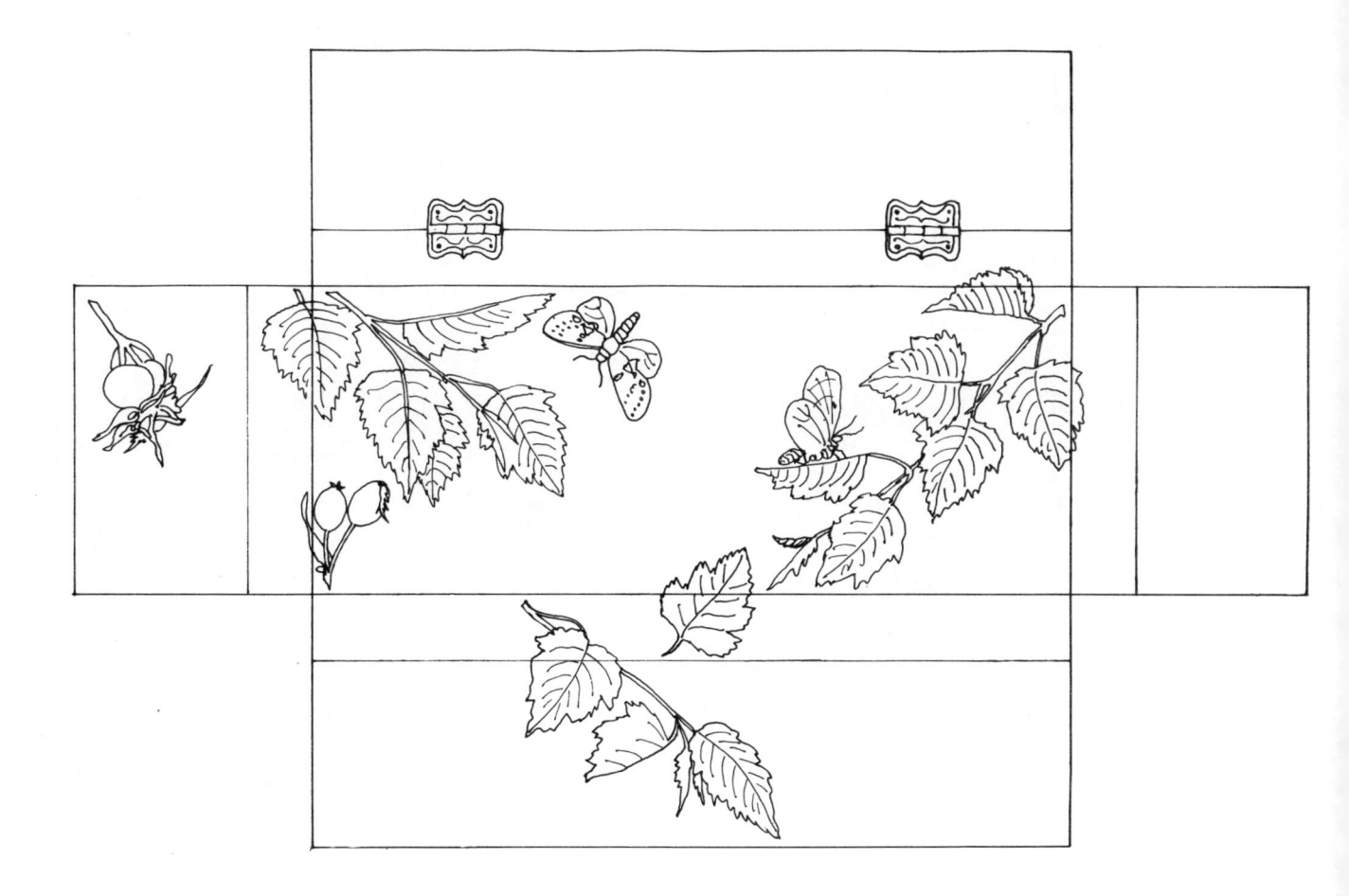

I think is the best for these green leaves and red berries. Try to overlap the designs on a box so that the cutouts flow from one side to the other making each side part of the other. The edge of the leaves hang from the top over onto the sides or from top to bottom. This gives the box a more complete look and makes it a bit more interesting than if I had placed a cutout on each side as an isolated design. It is a subtle thing that doesn't have to be very obvious.

Decoupage Designs

The look just created with leaves is very pretty and certainly doesn't seem like a beginner's project. But it is easy enough for a beginner and it can be considered finished as is. Yet more can also be done. Using print (※15) I cut out the dandelion and the black-eyed Susan as well as the trailing leaves. The grass blades are slivered from the long stem on print (※3 or 4). The flowers and leaves are placed so that they reach around the side of the box. The dandelion stretches up the front onto the top. Again an attractive, finished-looking design.

working with shapes

But you don't have to stop here either. You can go further. Add the red flower coming in from the top and place the orange butterfly going toward the flowers. You now have a balance of color and a very complete box. Looking at all three versions you can decide just how much work you want to do and the kind of look you want. Line the box with a bright orange paper or with black or green velvet to use as a jewelry box.

61

4. more ideas

LARGE OBJECTS

By the time you consider doing a large object you should be quite good at this designing business. It will take more than one print for most of the following projects. It takes more time to design a lap desk or a purse than to do a trinket box; however, it is no more difficult. With the small boxes you can cut out a print and design it easily. Sometimes the print covers the entire box. When you do a larger box it doesn't mean that you have to have a larger print to put on it. You just have to be a little more clever with your placement of each cutout design. Usually on a large object such as the ones here you have hinges and clasps as well as handles to deal with. Make them part of your design and work around them. When creating a decoupaged purse, use prints that will go with your outfits. Large objects of course show off more than small ones so when designing a project for your home consider where it will be used so that the design will fit with your room color and decor. Most of the decoupage prints are traditional in feeling and fit in anywhere. I find that most decoupage projects are easy to live with and if designed well should be at home in any environment.

Lap Desks

A lap desk can be used to hold writing papers, stamps, pens, and desk accessories. It can also be lined with velvet and used as a jewelry box. This is a most impressive project to work on because when finished you have a piece that can become an important object in a room. The first lap desk shown is quite simple to make because you are using print (#10) which is easy to cut. With a box this size you must be especially careful to do a good painting job since this will be quite noticeable. Use a small brush to get around hinges and clasps. Also paint the rim of the inside even if you are planning to line it. This box can be used on a desk in a den or office. The background is sand color. A mustard paint color or a wood stain would also make a very handsome background. I placed the tiger in the lower right-hand corner and not smack in the middle of the box, as it will look more unusual this way. When lining a box this size use a small print that will not overpower the design on the outside. Perhaps an over-all Early American print in a brown color can be found in a wallpaper sample.

The third cat in this print is placed on the inside lid. I have deliberately tried not to overdesign these lap desks so you can see that a simply appointed box can be just as lovely as one that uses many prints. You can also see that you don't need huge prints to do these projects.

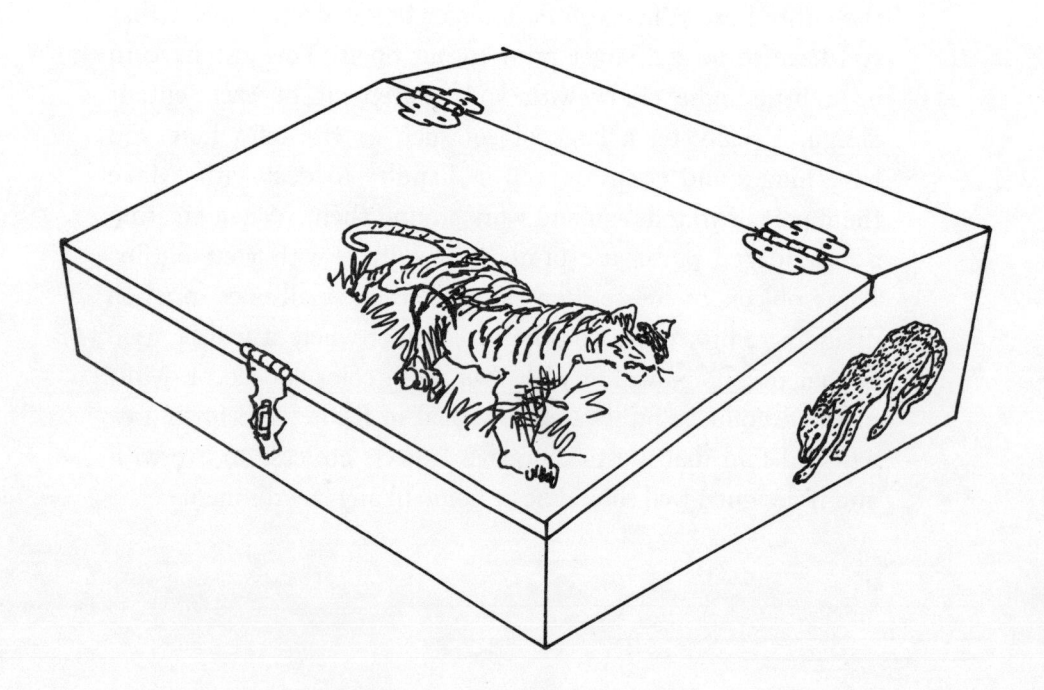

more ideas

The lap desk here uses prints (※24 and 25) and has a completely different look. Part of the flower was cut apart so that there was a piece to place around the hinge on the upper left. Also one of the flowers from the other plant was cut down and designed to go around the front clasp. When applying the large sprig on the right of the lap desk I bent the flower so that it "grows" around the hinge on the upper right. Notice also that the leaves to the right overlap onto the side and down onto the front of the box. The bird print (※22) is used on the inside cover. The background color used on this box is white.

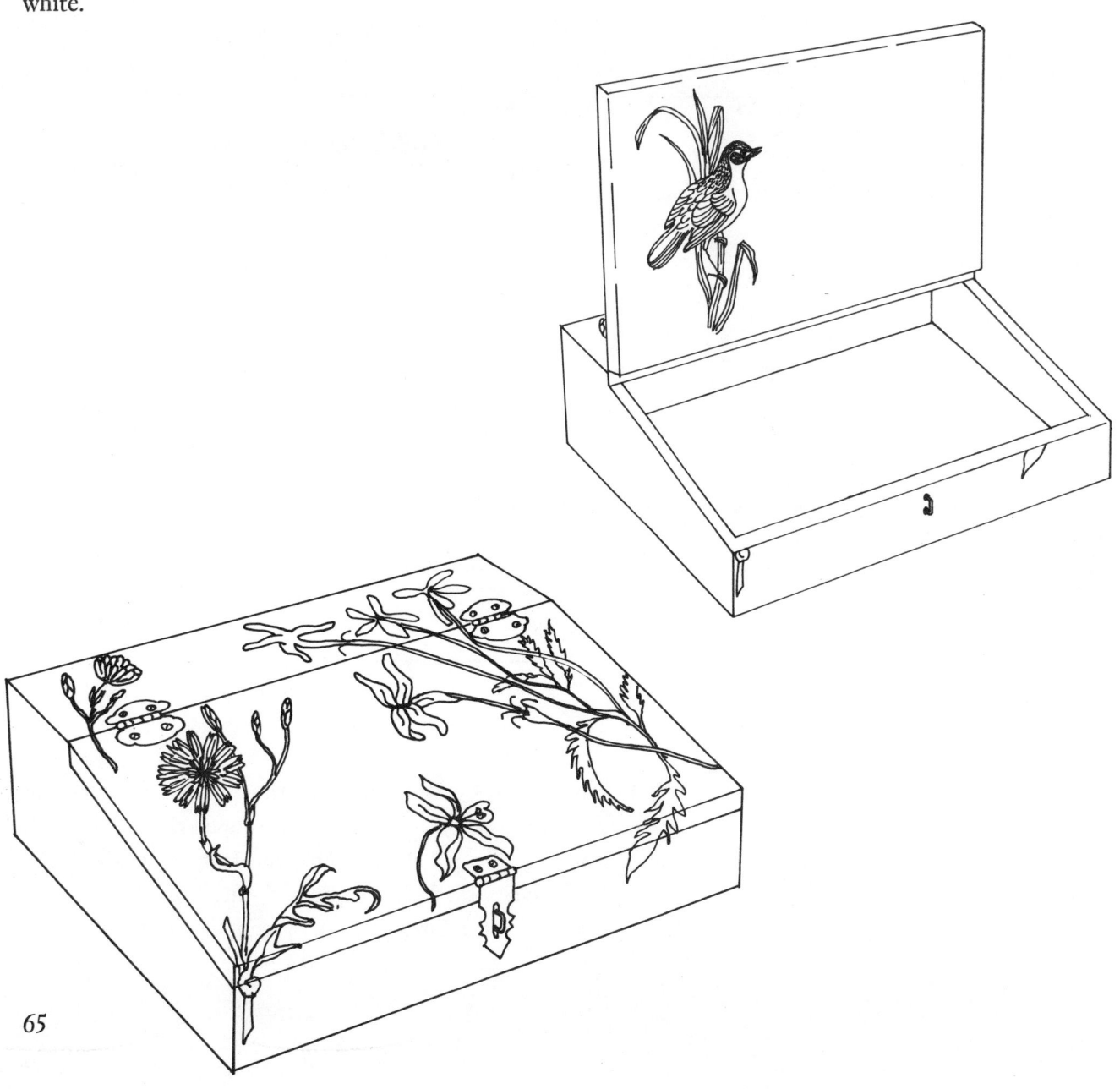

Decoupage Designs

The bird print (#22) is used this time on the front of the lap desk. Print (#23) is used on the upper right. The leaf comes from the top panel over onto the front just below the hinge. The leaves (#18) are combined with this design. The brown coloring of the birds with the green leaves makes a very

more ideas

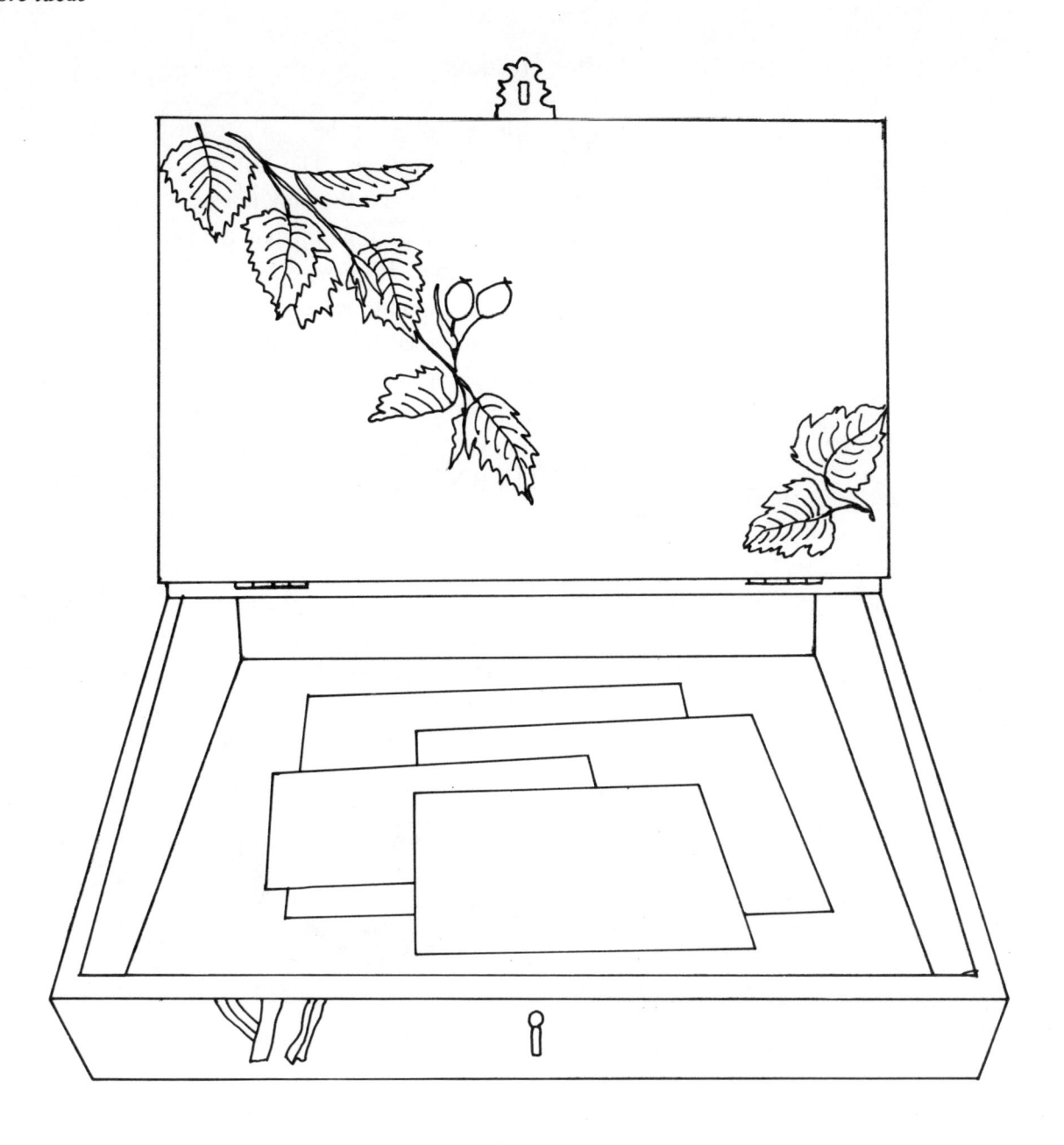

subtle design. The bottom part of the leaf branch that holds the butterfly was used around the hinge with one of the leaves extending over the edge onto the side. The rest of the leaves are used inside the lid. You can play around with this design, cutting apart the leaves and arranging them in different ways.

Letter Holders

These two letter boxes can be combined with the catchalls or a file box to make a desk set. The leaf design (#14) is on an ivory-white background and the pink flower design (#4) is on a blue background. The pink flower box is lined with a pink and gray marbleized paper. If these open boxes are lined with an unusual paper, they look especially nice even when not in use. There is a piece of green felt on the bottom of each to protect a desk top. Cut the piece of felt the exact size and spread glue over the entire bottom. Lay the felt piece down and stretch it to each side. Trim the excess with your cuticle scissors. Even if you line a box like this one, paint the top rim with a contrasting color.

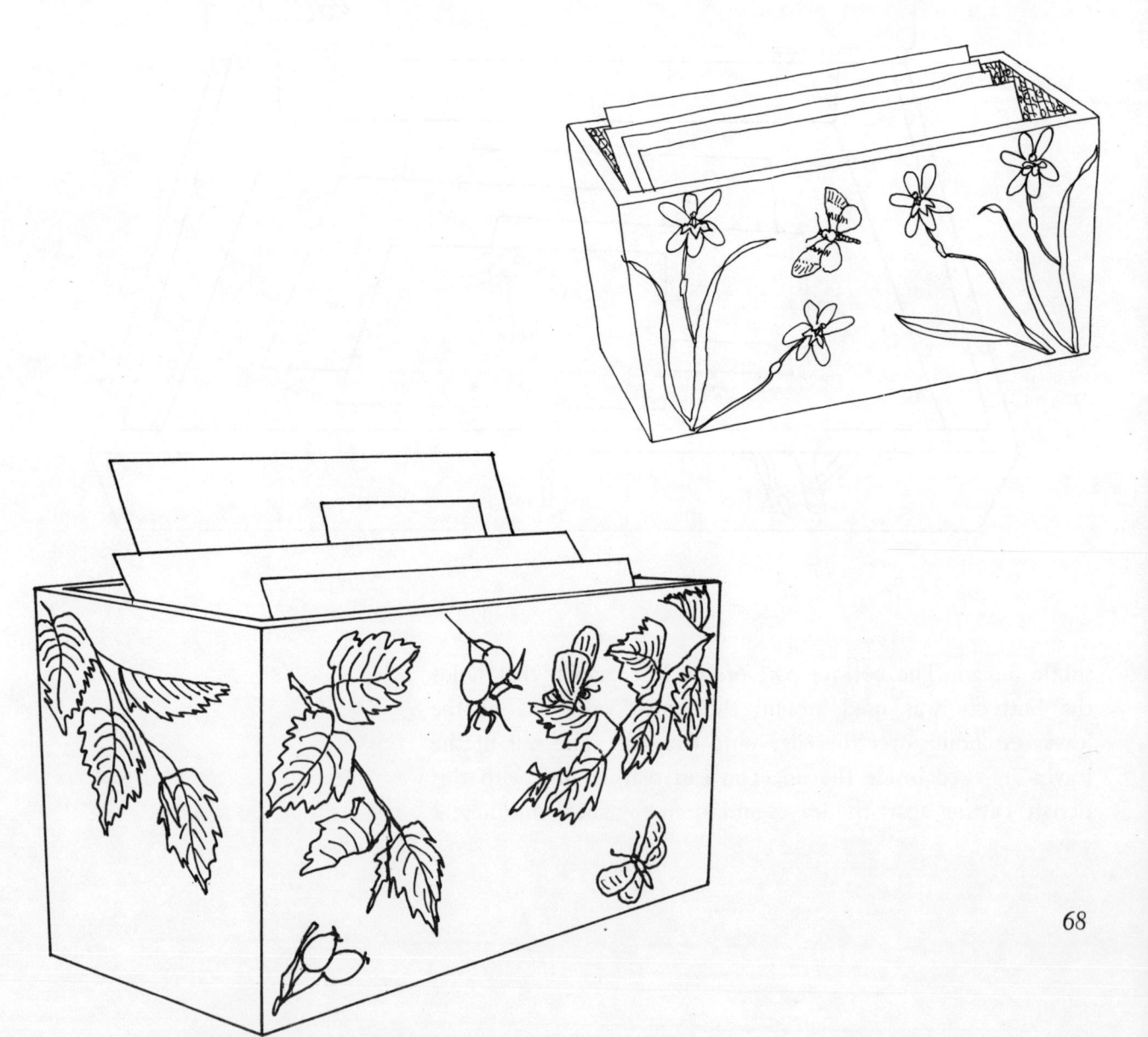

68

Wastebaskets

A wastebasket is a real challege. If it is square you must do all four sides and if it's round the design should extend all the way around. The wastebasket that I used is 9½ inches by 11

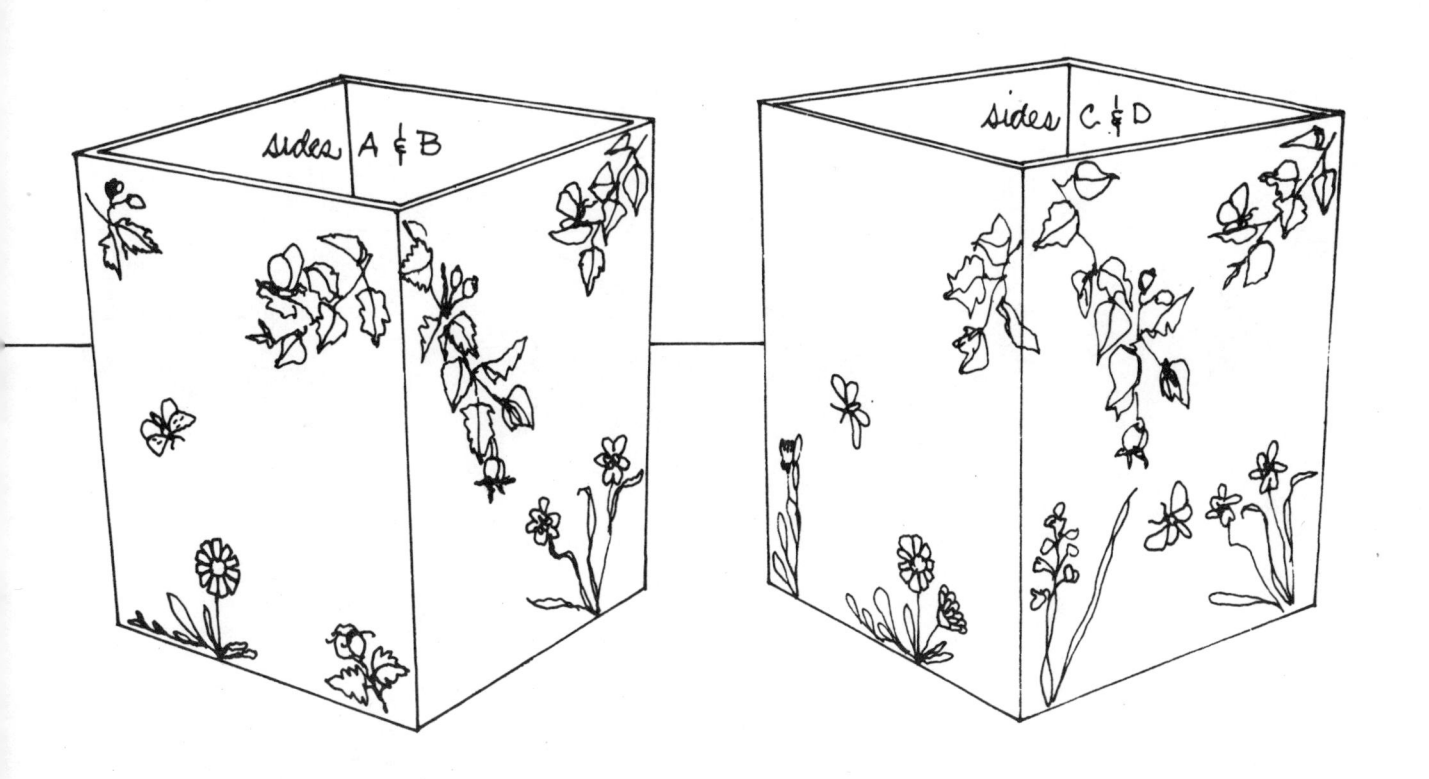

Decoupage Designs

inches high and is made of wood. I combined prints (※3 and 4, ※11 and 15, ※14 and 18). The background color is white and the inside is painted a moss green. If you are doing a wastebasket for a child's room you might like to add the characters from other prints (※13 and 17). One could be placed on each of the four sides. They would be walking around the bottom, so that the flowers are all larger, for a fantasy feeling.

A very good painting job on an object as large as this is vital if it is to look its best. Also when you varnish, it will probably take a pint of varnish to finish the job properly. When varnishing apply thin coats and be careful to let them dry thoroughly or you will have drip marks.

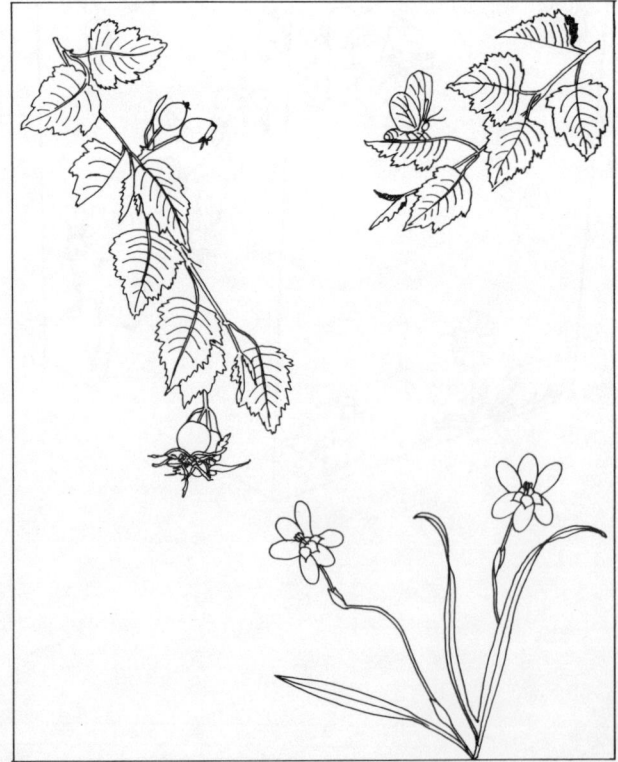

Purses

Purses have been a popular decoupage project for a long time. The following designs range from those that you are already familiar with to a few that will be much more time consuming. When working on a lacy design like the blue flowers the stems can easily tear when gluing. To avoid this cut it apart and glue each piece separately. Or, carefully apply a little bit of glue right on the object and then lay the cutout design on top of it. The reason I don't ordinarily do this is because if the glue dries too soon you will have a discoloration under the varnish. However, if you have a damp sponge ready to dab away glue as you go along you should be able to work this way. This is not the best way to apply the cutouts, but it can be done. You should dilute your glue slightly for these prints. Do not place the cutouts on a piece of paper while applying the glue. Use a surface like a kitchen counter. A piece of glass or a cutting board is also a good surface. This way your print won't stick to the paper when you lift it up.

Before gluing the cutouts in place lay each piece on the object. If it is a curved shape or a design that goes on the side, you can either tape it lightly or place a mark with a pencil on the object where the design should go. Spread the glue evenly with your fingertip, being sure the glue is spread to all outer edges. When the design is pressed firmly onto the piece, use your paintbrush handle to roll over the design. When decoupaging a curved or rounded piece it is especially important to double check that there are no air bubbles or excess glue trapped under the print. Rolling the design will prevent this.

The trunklike-shaped purses take two prints and sometimes three. The bright yellow buttercups (#5 and 7) are combined with the daisies (#16) which are used on the sides. One large flower is used on the front and the back. The background is an ivory color. Purses can be lined with a contrasting fabric. Trim around the inside rim with decorative ribbon or rickrack.

Using the pink flowers (#3 and 4) I spread them out on the front, back, and sides of this purse. For more coverage some leaves from other prints (#14 or 15) could be combined. This rectangular-shaped purse is decoupaged with prints (#6 and 8). The stems that appear to have been cut off at the bottom extend under the purse. The purple color of the iris and thistle go very well together on an off-white background with a touch of blue from the butterfly. The thistle was cut apart and the remaining piece is used to sprawl across the back from one corner down across the center. One butterfly was used on the back. The small purple butterfly could be placed on the top near the catch. A dark printed fabric would make an interesting lining.

15.

16.

17.

18.

20.

The Armillary Sphere

Plate XVIII.

21.

22.

23.

24. 25.

81

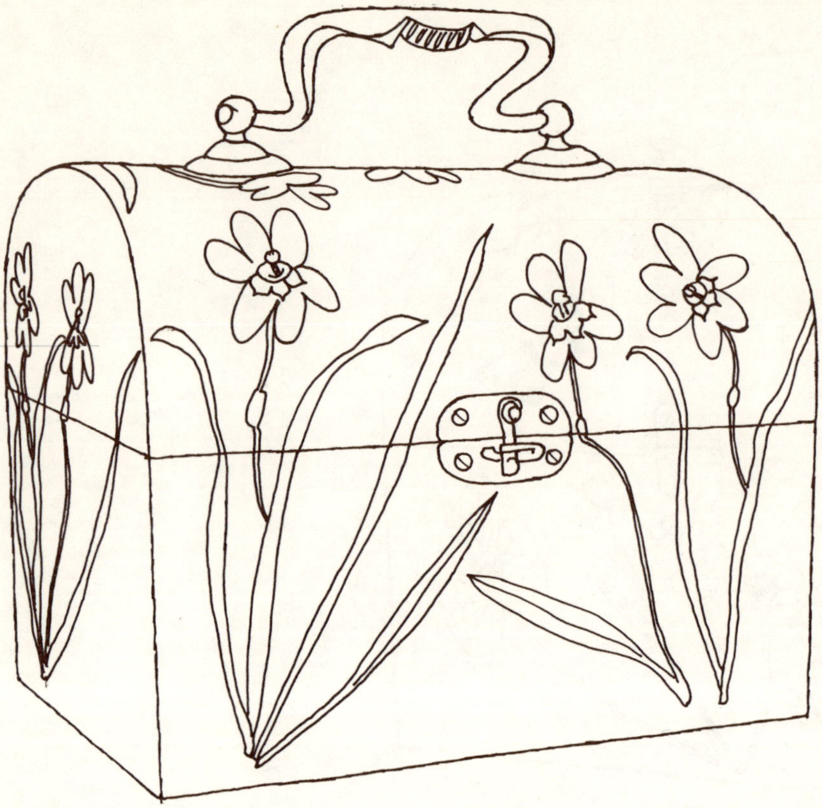

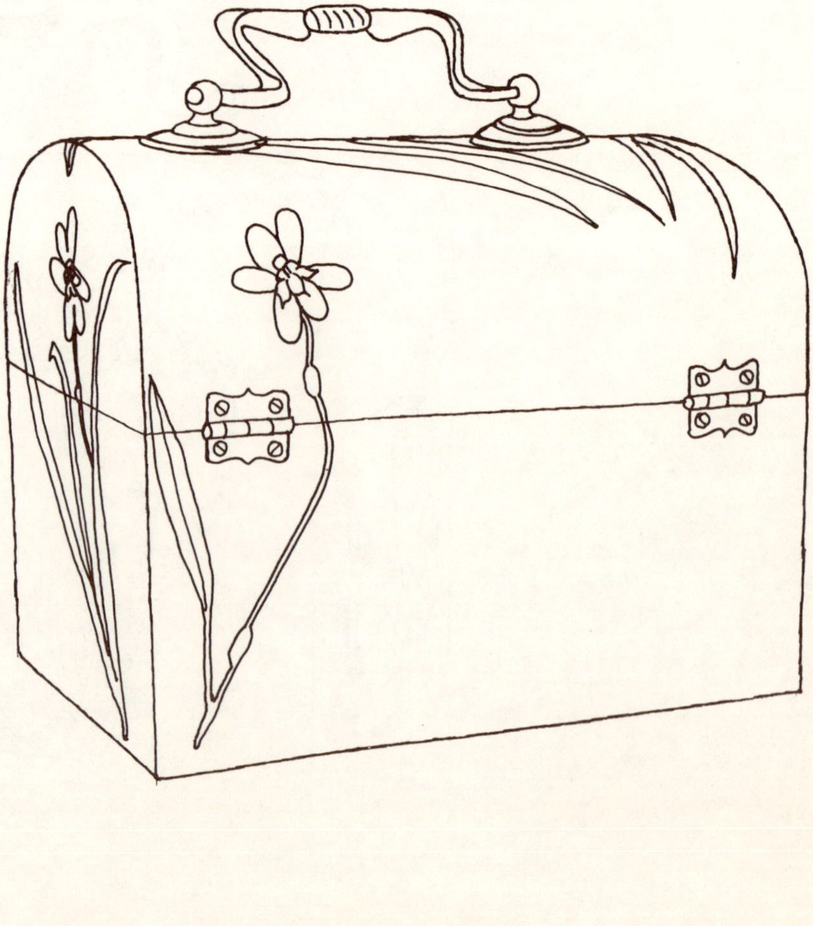

What Do You Do with a Pumpkin?

The pumpkin purse has been very popular. Most of them come with a print that wraps around the entire purse creating an over-all design. How can you do something to make your pumpkin purse original? I used the blue flower prints (#24 and 25) because of all the designs in the book these prints can be cut up and arranged in the most unique ways. Even if everyone who reads this book was to decoupage this purse using these prints the results would be entirely different.

Decoupage Designs

I used to teach a class on the *Queen Elizabeth 2*. My trinket box was a popular item with the sixty people in the class. Yet I often saw so many different versions of that box that I didn't think it was possible. Imagine what they could have done with these designs and box!

Rather than treating each panel separately, arrange the designs so that they overlap to the next panel. This will create a flowing design. I used the chicory print (#25) just as it is. Glued to the base of the purse, it extends up onto the top. The buds on the sides will extend to the next panels. I then cut the blue flower print (#24) apart so that I had a flower and leaves for each successive panel. If part of the flowers come up onto the top, this makes the top part of the whole design, rather than treating it as a separate piece.

SPECIAL PROJECTS

There are lots of odds and ends of items that are fun to try. Sometime you might want to make a little something to give as a gift. Or you may have children whom you are working with. It is great for them to have a project that is not too complicated, but that looks terrific when finished. I once made a small desk screen for *House Beautiful* magazine and many people wrote to me to find out how to design and make it. Again, "Where can I find the prints?" So here it is. A "no special category" section with special projects.

Some projects are not what I would call "designed." However, sometimes a print is just right as is on a particular object. This is true of these next three items.

more ideas

Humidor

It is often difficult to find a really beautiful print that can be used in an office as well as at home. This sphere print (※21) is simple, fits many objects round, square, and flat, and the color is neutral. I enjoyed using this print on a humidor and the catch-all. It has a border around it and can be used on a plaque of the same size. If you can't get a plaque the exact size, a local mill will cut one for you. If you use a board or box that is larger than the print, consider staining rather than painting it.

Breadboard

The bird print (#20) is a natural brown color and when placed on a wood background it couldn't look nicer. I wouldn't paint the background for this bird if possible. If you can find an object, such as the natural wood breadboard that I used, this is a lovely project. Use it to hang in a kitchen as a decoration and the reverse side can be used for cutting.

Tray

The bouquet print (#19) can be used on many different objects just as it is: a metal tray, a wooden bowl, perhaps on a small table, on the front of a dresser, or on a door. It is quite nice on a pale-blue background.

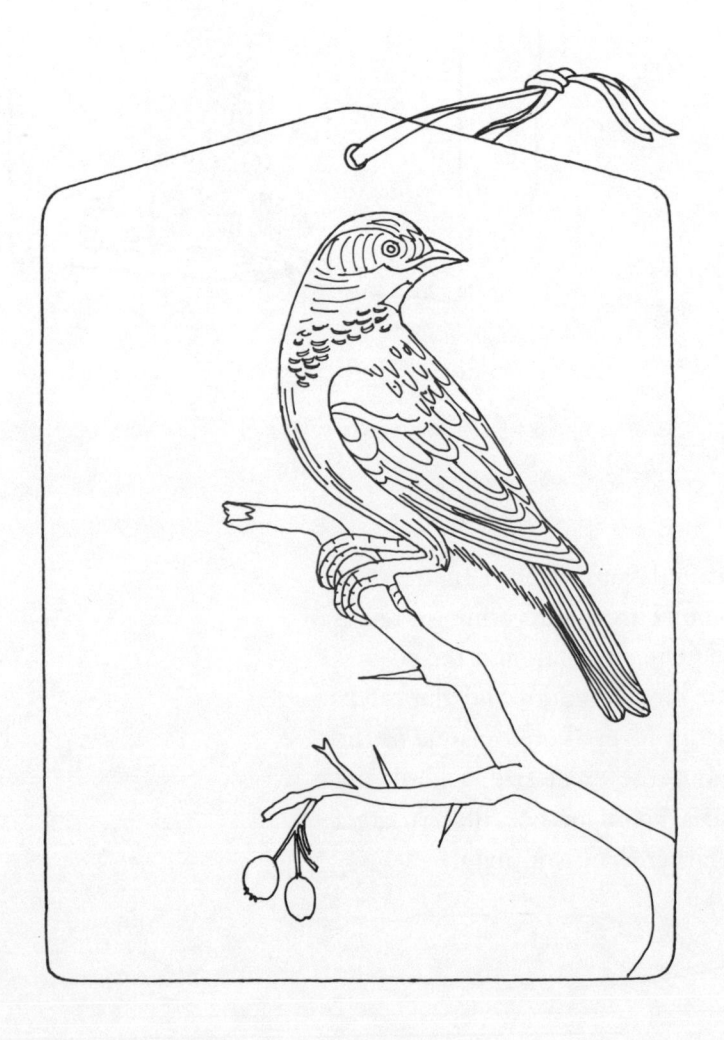

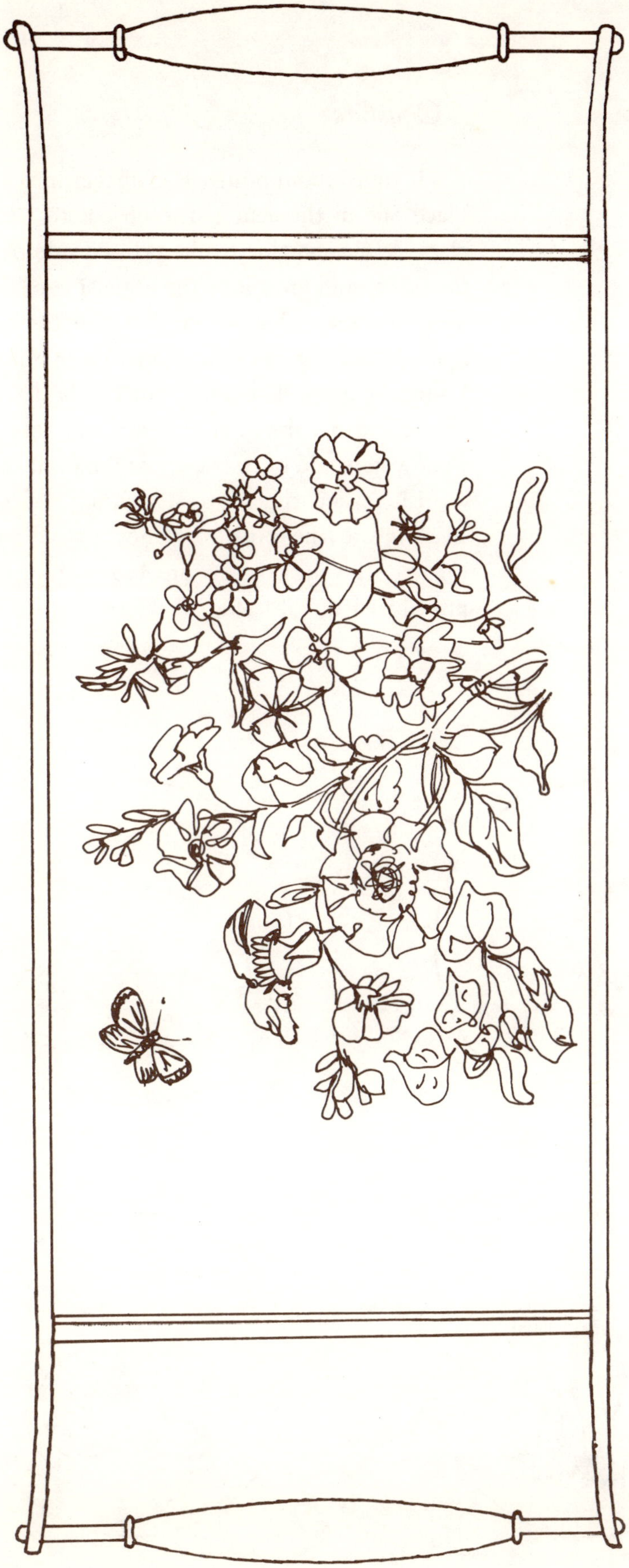

Coasters

The mushroom print (#1) makes into a good set of coasters. Place one in the center of each coaster. They can be made of glass. Apply the glue to the printed side of the mushroom (not the back) and press it to the underside of the glass. Pat it firmly until all excess glue is forced out of the sides. Choose a background color for the mushrooms. Sand color was used on these. Using a sponge, dab your paint on the back until the coaster is covered with paint. Let this dry and reapply. If the coaster is wood you would of course apply the print directly to the top and varnish several times over it. Other designs that are good for coasters are the pink rose hips (#9) and the small daisies (#16). If your coasters are too small for a print, adjust the print by cutting it to fit.

Flower Pots

The bird print (※23) is used on the front of a clay pot. When varnishing, you only have to cover the front where the design shows.

This is an old crock that was found in an antique store. I used the flower print (※19) just as it is. Cut it out so that the flowers show up nicely against a painted surface, but don't cut it apart. If you decide to use this print on a purse or piece of furniture it will probably stretch further if you cut it up. Design it to fit your object. Cut it apart where it seems natural, perhaps where stems overlap. Or you may want to cut leaves away and add them on elsewhere.

Screens

These three-paneled screens are miniature size for a desk top. They can be hinged or put together with cloth hinges between each panel. Glue each bird print (#23, 20, 22) to each of the three panels. Cut small pieces of leaves from another print (#18) and arrange them at the top of the screen so that the birds appear to be in the trees. Sand-colored paint is a good background for this scene.

more ideas

The bouquet print (※19) has been used exactly as it appears on a flat tray, a round crock, and now on a curved screen. It is an interesting and sophisticated print that can be pretty on all of these shapes. Trim the screen with a border of gold braid or decorative paper. A white background is used for this project.

91

Address Oval

When I had almost finished all the projects for this book I decided to give myself a real challenge. You might try this project if you have been doing decoupage for some time and feel comfortable with it. I chose the thistle print (#6), which is rather stiff, and wanted to use it on an oval plaque. I cut the print apart every way possible and began placing the different parts on this curved shape. It was most frustrating. It just wouldn't work, and I put it aside for days. Later I decided I couldn't give up, so I took out the cutouts and stuck with it for about two hours until I felt I had achieved a good composition. Of course it's easier if you use a more obvious combination of object and print right off, but don't get discouraged if your idea for using a print doesn't work immediately. Now and then a challenge can be interesting.

Candlesticks

Using part of a print can bring new ideas; for example, in prints (※24 and 25), the blue flowers are delicate enough for candlesticks. I used only a small part of each design. By cutting the stems shorter and adding a leaf from farther down you can re-create a flower that fits the object. This leaves you with enough undestroyed flowers for something else. If you are careful when cutting up a design, there is always more that can be used. Even stems can and should be saved. You never know when you will need to lengthen a stem.

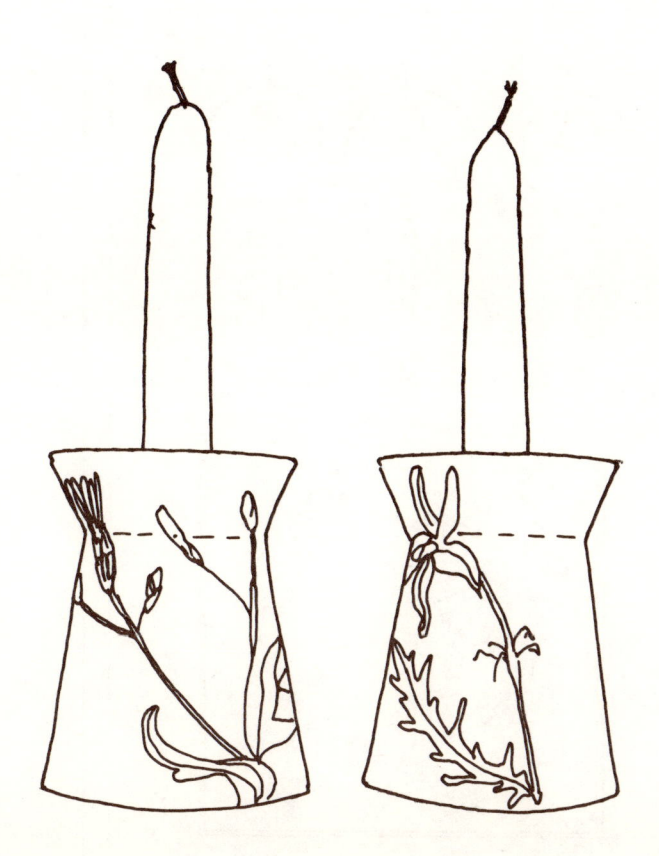

Just For Kids

Most of the easier projects like the cosmetic cup and the trinket box are good for children as well as adults. But really young children need a project that can be done quickly and very easily. This one requires very little cutting and can be done in about a half hour. The key holder is made from a block of wood and the print is the hen (※17). The rabbit (※13), the wedding couple (※17), or one of the animals (※10) could be used. The frog is too tall unless you use a large rectangular shape. This print is cut out, pasted in place, and a border can be added with paint. The hooks for the keys are cup hooks that are easily screwed into the board. A couple of coats of varnish completes a satisfying project for a child to give as a gift or to hang in the kitchen.

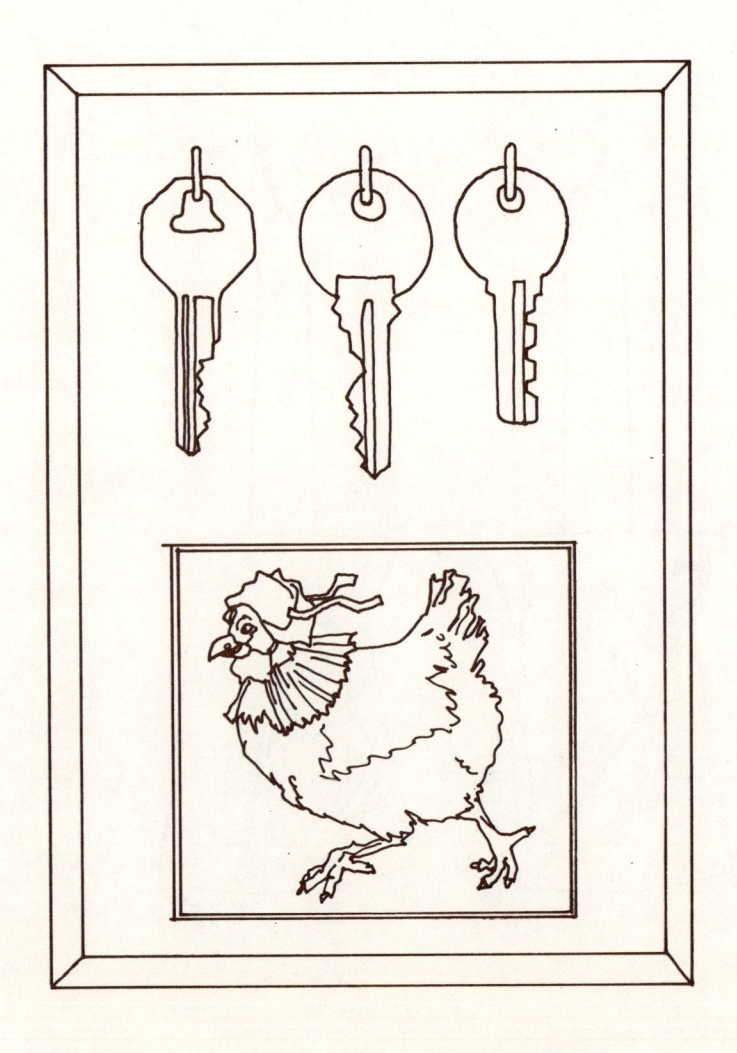

more ideas

Cans can also be decoupaged as pencil holders.

I didn't leave Ms. Frog out (※13). She makes a fine design on the catchall that can hold magic markers. Green paint is a good background color against her blue outfit.

The little cosmetic cup is the easiest project of all. Cut the stems down so that the buttercups (※7) fit and extend them up over the rim. This makes the best crayon holder and is even easier to design with mushrooms.

Now that I've presented my ideas for projects and decoupage designs I hope that you can become more creative by designing some of your own. I know it's very tempting to plunge right in and begin with an involved project, but remember, if you don't

Decoupage Designs

finish you will never have the satisfaction of the completed piece. Try to start slowly and you'll be surprised at how each new project gets better and better. I often look at some boxes that I did ages ago and wonder how I ever decided to do it that way. The longer you take to select your final design the more confident you'll feel about it. This is not to say that it should become tedious, but it is worth taking time to do well.

Decoupage is fun and can give you a great feeling of creative satisfaction. You don't need lots of space, money, or even time. Best of all you don't need any formal training. So enjoy decoupage and keep looking for new prints to add to what you have from the book. If there are any problems that you can't solve, or you've had a great experience and a project has turned out to be super, I always welcome a note from my readers.